THE RUSSIAN REVOLUTIONS

For many years before the Communists came to power there were periodic attempts to break the autocratic rule of the Czars of Russia. Sometimes the revolutionaries were intellectuals, sometimes even members of the nobility, and sometimes people from some of the provinces that wanted to break free of Russia. The author has compiled the history of Russia by depicting the people responsible for the important revolutions: Catherine the Great, Nicholas I, Alexander II, Rasputin. The more familiar Russian leaders are also included: Lenin, Kerensky, Stalin, as well as the battles prior to the important revolutions.

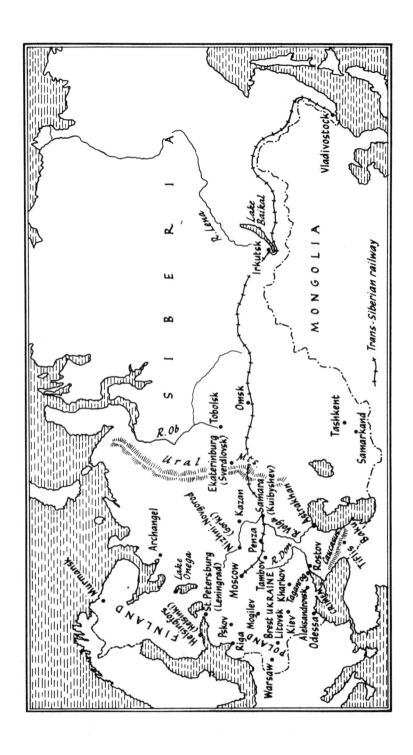

The Russian Revolutions

by David Footman

G. P. Putnam's Sons   New York

Contents

THE RUSSIAN REVOLUTIONS

CHAPTER I

Russia As It Was

R ussia has always been something apart from the rest of Europe. It is an enormous country; Vladivostock on the Pacific is six thousand miles from what was then the Russo-German frontier, and it is nearly three thousand miles from the Arctic Sea to the Persian frontier in the south.

There are high mountain ranges along the southern frontiers; and a chain of low hills, the Ural Mountains, separates European Russia from Siberia. Otherwise the country is one huge plain. Over most of the area the climate is harsh, with long and bitterly cold winters. In the north there are thousands of square miles where the soil is frost-bound all the year round and where in the short summers the swarms of gnats and mosquitoes make work in the open painful and difficult. Much of the north is covered with the largest forests in the world, and much of the rest is steppes, great treeless plains.

Parts of south and central Russia are very fertile, but in

9

other parts the soil is often poor. Certain areas are rich in natural resources — coal, oil, iron ore and other minerals — but a hundred years ago not many mines were being worked. At that time there were few railways, and the unpaved roads turned into bogs in the autumn rains and when the snows melted in the spring. Much of the traffic went, and still goes, along the great slow-flowing rivers.

The country was sparsely populated — there were far fewer people to the square mile than in England, France or Germany. Most of them were peasants, living in isolated villages, and for most of the peasants the standard of living was very low. In parts of the country the soil was poor, and where the soil was good there were often so many people crammed into the village that there was not enough to go around.

There were some very rich landowners with huge estates and there were a few rich businessmen — mostly in the capital, Petersburg (founded by Peter the Great in 1703), in Moscow, the old capital, and in some of the big provincial towns. But, on the whole, Russia was a poor country, and, compared to western Europe, very backward. There were few hospitals and very few schools. As late as 1897 only one in four of the population could read and write.

Russia was an autocracy, which meant that the ruler of Russia, the Emperor, or Czar, held supreme and absolute power. There was no Parliament and no general elections. There were ministers in charge of the various government departments, but the Emperor appointed them and dismissed them as he wished, just as he appointed and dismissed the governors of the various provinces.

The Russian people had no say in how the government was run. The day-to-day business of government, collecting taxes, keeping order and so on, was all in the hands of an army of officials working under the various ministries. It was not a very efficient system. The rules and regulations were sometimes broken or ignored when the officials felt there was no danger of their getting into trouble. Some of them took bribes — the lower ranks were so badly paid that they could not keep their families unless they made some money on the side.

All Russians were officially divided into classes — nobles, merchants, small townsmen and peasants. Your class was entered on the passport which you had to carry when traveling about the country.

The nobles had a number of privileges — such as not having to do military service. Nobility was hereditary. If your father was noble you were noble yourself and enjoyed a noble's privileges. You could also become a noble by reaching a certain rank in the army or in the civil service. The father of Lenin became a noble when he was made Chief Inspector of Schools.

But most nobles belonged to landowning families. A few were enormously rich, with huge estates; far more of them had only small properties and if the land was poor, or if, as so often, it was badly farmed, they got into debt with the banks and the money-lenders.

The merchant class grew in numbers and wealth during the second half of the nineteenth century, when more factories were built and business developed. But they had little interest in anything outside their own business and home affairs. And it was the same with the small townsmen, who were petty traders, craftsmen and artisans.

Numerically, by far the largest class in Russia was that of the peasants. They were a people apart — indeed they were sometimes known as and sometimes called themselves "The Dark People." Up to 1861 most of them were serfs, attached either to the State and Imperial domains or to the properties of private landowners. They were bought and sold with the estate they lived on — in fact a common way of describing a property was to say it consisted of so many "souls" rather than of so many acres.

These serfs were in the power of their masters, who could have them flogged for petty offenses. They were bound to the estates and could not leave without permission. Permission was seldom granted, because the landlords wanted their labor, and the government wanted them there to pay taxes and provide recruits for the army.

Sometimes they ran away, hoping to find a free life in the vast empty spaces of Siberia or along the southern frontiers. But if caught they were brought back again and severely punished.

The peasants were ignorant, backward and miserably poor. Mostly they bore with their lot, but on some occasions they took to violence. In the 1770's there was a peasant revolt in southeast Russia under one Pugachev, who pretended to the rightful Emperor.

Hundreds of thousands of peasants came to join him, killing the landlords and their families and burning their country houses. The revolt was suppressed by the army, but for many years afterwards the ruling classes were terrified at what might happen if liberty were granted to the serfs.

In an autocracy, a great deal depends on the character of the autocrat[1]; and a great deal too depends upon the little circle round the autocrat who can advise him on what he should do.

Throughout the nineteenth century, the advisers of the Emperor of Russia were of two kinds. Some were *liberals* (see the note in the glossary) who wanted the people to have more say in the business of government and to let Russia develop along the lines of the more up-to-date Western countries.

The others, the conservatives, held that the Russian autocracy with its class system and its serfdom had been ordained by God and must be maintained exactly as it was. They thought that Russians were not suited for self-government and that to grant them liberty would only lead to chaos.

The various emperors sometimes listened to one set of advisers and sometimes to the other.

[1] Political expressions like *autocrat* are explained in the glossary at the end of the book.

The German princess who reigned over Russia from 1762 to 1796 was a woman of great intelligence and force of character who fully deserved her title of Catherine the Great. But her son Paul was mentally abnormal; he was murdered, unmourned, in a Palace revolution in 1801.

The next Emperor, Alexander I, was on the throne eleven years later when Napoleon invaded Russia, got as far as Moscow, and then had to retreat again through the bitter cold and snows of a Russian winter, losing most of his *Grand Armée* before he reached France. Alexander I had, at one time, ideas of reform, and the liberals were encouraged. But these plans came to nothing, and towards the end of his reign the would-be reformers began to plot against him.

He died in 1825 and was succeeded by his brother Nicholas I, whose first act was to suppress the Decembrist Revolt (of which more in the next chapter). Nicholas was a thoroughgoing conservative, and had no use for reformers and liberals.

He was interested in police work and did much to build up a special political police force whose task it was to ferret out and suppress any beginnings of opposition to the government régime. Incidentally, secret political police work has played an important part in any government of Russia ever since. Under the Czars the force was called the *Okhrana*; and when the Bolsheviks came to power they established a force of their own, the *Cheka,* with even more drastic methods and far-reaching powers.

Under Nicholas I any open opposition was effectively suppressed. But discontent was growing. And though, outwardly, the régime was stable and imposing, there was much in Russia that was out of date and inefficient. When the Crimean War broke out in 1854, and British and French troops landed in south Russia, the Russian supply and transport services broke down; so there came the humiliation of Russian armies being defeated by foreigners on Russian soil. Discontent grew more and more bitter. When Nicholas died, in early 1855, there was everywhere a feeling that drastic changes were bound to come.

And indeed the new Emperor, Alexander II, did succeed in carrying through a number of important reforms. The first was the abolition of serfdom, in 1861, a measure designed to ensure that millions of Russian peasants should no longer live in conditions of semi-slavery. Other reforms were concerned with the law courts, with the army, with education and with the setting up of district councils to help with local government.

Freeing the serfs was a great step forward, but soon people were saying the decree did not go far enough. It is true the peasants were no longer the property of their landlords, but they were still bound to stay in their villages, so that the authorities could collect taxes from them and call them up for military service.

Moreover most peasants wanted land more than they wanted liberty, and the way the land was divided up after the decree of 1861 meant that a lot of them had smaller plots than they had before. Besides, the land was only given them on a sort of time payment, with installments to be paid off over a number of years. As a result of the liberation quite a number of peasants were actually poorer.

So the reforms had a mixed reception. Old-fashioned people said they went too far. Reformers said they did not go far enough. The more ardent spirits formed secret or *underground* groups with the idea of forcing the government to make further concessions. Some of them, mostly very young people, thought that violence or terrorist action might frighten the authorities into giving way.

Attempts were made on the life of the Emperor. All this bewildered Alexander, conscious of his sincere desire to do the best for his people. "What have they got against me?" he asked. "Why do they hunt me down like a wild beast?"

Early in 1881 the Emperor was considering a plan for a constitution for Russia, which would allow for a sort of parliament. But, on March 1st, as he was driving through the streets of Petersburg a young revolutionary threw a bomb which exploded under his carriage. The Emperor was horribly mutilated and taken back to his Palace, where he died a few hours later. All the family were gathered round his deathbed; there was his son, who succeeded him as Alexander III, and a little boy of twelve, his grandson, who was in due course to come to the throne as Nicholas II and who never forgot the horror of his grandfather's last hours.

Of course this assassination put an end to any thought of

liberal reforms. Alexander III was a great strong bullock of a man, like an old-fashioned sergeant major, both in looks and character. The young revolutionaries were hunted down by the secret police; some were executed, some died in prison or in exile in Siberia. The policy of the Emperor and his advisers was to suppress all opposition and all attempts at reform; and the design of the education of his son and heir to the throne was to ensure that he too would rule Russia as an old-fashioned autocrat.

Young Nicholas had a Spartan upbringing. He slept on a hard bed, got up every morning at six, and soon was taught riding and military drill. He was a gentle, kindly boy, who grew up to look very like his cousin, King George V of England. He was devoted to country life and country sports and took his military training very seriously. When he was twenty-one, a German princess of seventeen came on a visit to Petersburg, and Nicholas fell violently in love with her.

Princess Alix of Hesse-Darmstadt was, like so many royalties of that time, a granddaughter of Queen Victoria. She had spent a number of years at Kensington Palace in London, and she and Nicholas spoke English (not always very correctly) when they were together. At first Nicholas was afraid that he might never be able to marry her. His mother did not approve of the match; and, what was even more important, the wife of the heir to the throne had to belong to the official Russian Orthodox Church, and Princess Alix, as a German princess, was a Lutheran Protestant.

It was a five-year courtship, but at last, in April 1894, the princess agreed to change her faith, and the betrothal was officially announced. On November 1st, the Emperor Alexander died and Nicholas came to the throne. Five weeks later he married Princess Alix. The ceremonies included a mass distribution of presents to the crowd. The affair was mismanaged, there was a general stampede and a number of people were crushed to death. It was in no way the young Emperor's fault — he was not even there at the time. But it was felt to be a bad omen for the beginning of his reign.

In one of his first speeches Nicholas declared that he would rule Russia as an autocrat as firmly as his father had done. But times were changing and autocracy was getting more and more out of date. By the turn of the century, industry in Russia had greatly developed; and the factory workers wanted to form trade unions and secure better wages and working conditions. In spite of all the efforts of the police, two revolutionary parties came into being underground, that is to say in secret: the Social Democrats, mostly concerned with the workers, and the Socialist Revolutionaries, or SRs, concerned with the peasants. We shall have more to say about these parties in the next chapter. And a middle-class opposition party was shortly to come into being — the Constitutional Democrats (or Cadets) who wanted a constitutional government with a parliament as in Britain or France.

It would have needed a greater man than Nicholas to overcome all his difficulties. He had some able ministers, but he did not trust them and would find some pretext to get rid of them: Perhaps his idea of autocracy made him dislike giving wide powers to anyone abler than himself.

And, conscientious as he was, it does not seem that he really liked the business of government.

What he enjoyed was to be with his family on one of his country estates. He and the Empress were a devoted couple. For the Empress, her whole life was bounded by her husband, her family and her religion. She did not like the pomp and ceremony of court life. With strangers she was shy and awkward, and this made her unpopular. Another and quite unjust reason for her unpopularity was that for years she did not have a son. Four daughters came, one after the other, but it was not till 1904 that an heir to the throne was born. And then there came a new anxiety. It was found that the little Czarevitch suffered from hemophilia — an affliction of the blood that meant that if he ever cut himself there was a risk that he might bleed to death.

The year 1904 was a momentous one for Russia. War broke out with Japan in the Far East. It was a war that Nicholas might well have avoided had he listened to the right advisers. The war went on for eighteen months and Russia suffered defeat after defeat. As a final effort the Russian Home Fleet was sent more than halfway round the world from the Baltic to the Pacific: Off the island of Tsushima it met the Japanese Fleet and was destroyed in forty minutes.

All this time the uncertainties, frustrations and humiliations of the war were sharpening the discontents at home. Liberals, peasants, workers became more and more restive.

On January 22, 1905, an enormous crowd of workers with their wives and families, led by an Orthodox priest, Father Gapon, marched on the Winter Palace in Petersburg to present a petition to the Emperor. The troops on guard at the Palace lost their heads and opened fire: Altogether five hundred men, women and children were killed and thousands more wounded. The anger and horror aroused by this massacre of Bloody Sunday was the prelude to what came to be known as the Revolution of 1905.

It was not an organized revolution. The leaders of the revolutionary parties (mostly abroad to be out of the reach of the Russian police) did not at first realize what was happening. And it would be hard to say exactly when it began. In June there was a mutiny in the battleship *Potemkin* in the Black Sea Fleet. All over Russia angry peasants started looting and burning their landlords' houses. In late July revolutionary exiles and their Western sympathizers chartered a small steamer, the S.S. *John Grafton*, to carry arms to the insurgents, but the ship ran aground off the Finnish coast. In the early autumn the trouble spread to the towns. There was a printers' strike in Moscow. Then the railway workers struck.

Very soon almost everybody stopped work. There were no newspapers, no mail, no streetcars. The banks shut down. Even the *corps de ballet* came out on strike. Representatives of the factory workers and revolutionary groups met together and formed a *Soviet*, a general council, which acted as a sort of army headquarters to direct the strikes and to organize and encourage active opposition to the government. One of its leaders was Trotsky, who was to play so prominent a part in the later revolution.

The Emperor became seriously alarmed. In October, reluctantly and under pressure from his ministers, he issued a declaration or manifesto promising Russia a constitution. The proposals left too much power in the Emperor's hands to please the liberals — let alone the revolutionaries — but it did in a way mark a turning-point. Opposition became weaker. The strikers gradually went back to work: Otherwise they could not have bought food for themselves and their families.

There were still ugly incidents. The troops coming back from the Japanese war were restless and undisciplined, and there was trouble in a number of garrisons both in Russia proper and in the Russian Far East. There were more naval mutinies, at Kronstadt, the naval base off Petersburg, and in the Black Sea Fleet. In certain provinces the peasants went on looting and burning. But gradually the government gained the upper hand. The Petersburg Soviet was suppressed, and Trotsky and others arrested. A revolt in Moscow (where the revolutionaries had got hold of arms and put up barricades in the streets) was crushed when the authorities brought up artillery. By early 1906 the police and the loyal troops were in full control.

A good deal happened in Russia between 1906 and 1914, but so much more happened later that the earlier period has been overlooked. The reforms promised in the Emperor's October Manifesto were to some extent brought into being. A parliament or *Duma* was elected. Local government was developed, and good work was done towards providing the much-needed hospitals and schools in the country districts. The censorship was eased, and a lot was published that would never have been allowed before.

In 1909 a very able Prime Minister, Stolypin, brought in new land measures to enable the more hard-working peasants to become prosperous yeoman farmers. It was a time of rapid industrial growth, with new factories and new railways, that brought greater prosperity to many. It was a time, too, that saw a marked decline in the influence and activity of the underground revolutionary parties. Many began to hope that there was now a chance to build up a freer and happier Russia by legal means, so that there was little point in the oldtime plots and conspiracies.

But before long discontent began to increase again, as had happened after the Great Reforms of the 1860's. The Emperor and his conservative advisers thought he had given away too much in the way of reforms. The liberals and the opposition generally thought he had not given enough.

The first Duma or Parliament was dissolved after two months of angry quarrels between the liberal majority and the Emperor's government. Though the subsequent Dumas were elected on a different system, designed to bring in more government supporters, the angry quarrels persisted.

Meanwhile outside the Duma the more determined revolutionaries were plotting and organizing underground. There were assassinations of leading officials. There was a plot (which miscarried) to kill the Emperor when he came on board a new battleship: The ship was being built in a Glasgow shipyard, and revolutionary agents, under false names, visited Glasgow to make their preparations. There were a number of daring raids on State banks by armed gangs of revolutionaries to get money for their organizations. Perhaps even more important were the efforts of the revolutionaries to increase their influence over the workers, who, by 1912, numbered two and a half million.

As we have seen, the Emperor was not the man himself to solve big problems, or to choose and support ministers who could solve them on his behalf. Stolypin, of course, was extremely able, but in 1911 he was shot at and killed by a terrorist in his box at the theatre in Kiev. The following Prime Ministers — and there was a whole series of them — were all lesser men.

During this time the Emperor and his family were tending to get out of touch with the people over whom they ruled. The Empress, as we know, did not like court life. As she grew older she retired more and more into a circle of not always well-chosen intimates. From about 1903 she came increasingly under the influence of a certain Rasputin.

Rasputin was a peasant from Siberia. He wore a long black cassock which made foreigners think he was a priest, but he had never been ordained. Like many others then in Russia he would wander from place to place, living on alms and offering prayers for the sick and afflicted. Someone told the Empress his prayers might help her little son, and so he was brought to the Palace.

Rasputin was quite uneducated. He was careful to behave when with the Empress, but in private life he was dirty, drunken and dissolute. He had considerable cunning, and what is more, possessed hypnotic powers, especially with regard to the Czarevitch. It used to happen that when the boy seemed to be bleeding to death and the doctors helpless, Rasputin would appear at his bedside or send a message and the little prince would get better.

The Empress, who was very religious, came to regard the man as God's chosen instrument to preserve the life of her son, and furthermore, the channel for divine guidance as to how her beloved husband should rule his Empire. And she would impress upon the Emperor any suggestions that Rasputin made as to what he ought to do and whom he should appoint as ministers.

Of course people in court and government circles were very angry over Rasputin's interference in state affairs. And then there was his scandalous behavior: for instance, he would go to a nightclub, get very drunk and start taking his clothes off. Stolypin banished him from Petersburg; the next Prime Minister ordered a full inquiry. But the devotion of the Empress (who would believe nothing against him) and her influence on her husband were too much for Rasputin's enemies, and long before war broke out he was back in his old position.

World War I broke out on August 1, 1914. Few people in Russia understood the causes of the war, or realized the dangers it involved. But the outbreak of war called forth a tremendous wave of patriotic emotion. Crowds surged along the streets singing "God save the Tsar"; the German Embassy was sacked. The former German-sounding name of Petersburg was Russianized into Petrograd. The quarrels in the Duma seemed forgotten overnight. Strikes were abandoned and workers and peasants thronged in to answer the call to war. All were confident of a speedy and glorious victory. For the moment it seemed that the Emperor and his people were at last united.

CHAPTER II

The Revolutionary Movement

It would be hard to say when the Russian revolutionary movement first started. In 1790, by some oversight of the censor, there appeared a book, *A Journey from Petersburg to Moscow*, which exposed the sufferings of the serfs and attacked the way in which Russia was being ruled. The Empress Catherine was horrified when it came to her notice; the French Revolution was then taking place in France, and it seemed to the Empress that the book was a call for a revolution in Russia. The author was arrested and exiled to Siberia, and the police destroyed all the copies of the book they could find.

But *A Journey* was only a book. The first attempt at an actual revolt was not to come till more than thirty years later. The Decembrists, as these first conspirators were later called (because their revolt took place in December) were young officers of noble family who had been with the army outside Russia during the Napoleonic wars. They had noticed how much better off than the Russian serfs were the peasants in France and other Western countries. They were affected, too, by Western books about equality and freedom and by what had happened in England, America and France. They formed groups to discuss their ideas in secret; and when they saw that the Emperor Alexander did not intend to grant reforms they grew more and more convinced that they should act.

They never worked out an agreed program. Some wanted to kill the Emperor and proclaim a republic. Some wanted a constitutional monarchy as in the West. Some aimed at appointing one of their number as dictator with supreme power. Furthermore they never succeeded in building up a properly disciplined organization. By 1825 there were two main wings of the movement — the Northern Society based in Petersburg and the Southern Society in and around Kiev. But they did not work closely together.

The Emperor Alexander I had been warned some time before about what was going on. But he took no action. He did not believe that these young men were likely to do anything serious. It was only on his deathbed that he received more detailed reports showing the extent of the conspiracy.

He died at Taganrog in south Russia in November, 1825. There followed one of the most curious episodes in Russian history.

Alexander had no son, and his natural heir would have seemed to be his brother, Grand Duke Constantine, who was then in Warsaw. But Constantine never wanted to be Emperor, and Alexander in 1822 (three years before he died) signed a secret order naming another brother, Nicholas, to succeed him as Emperor.

But he kept this order very secret, and Nicholas did not even know that it existed. And so when news reached Petersburg that Alexander was dead, Nicholas at once swore an oath of allegiance to Constantine and made the senior officials and officers do the same.

His mother, the Dowager Empress, knew of the secret order. But when she heard of Alexander's death she fainted and did not recover till after the oath of allegiance had been taken.

There was great excitement in the top Palace circles. The secret order was brought out and read. But all the same Nicholas persisted that Constantine and not himself must be Emperor.

Couriers were urgently sent to Constantine in Warsaw. But Constantine was adamant in his refusal to succeed to the throne; in fact he threatened to leave Russia and go abroad. So that in the end, nearly three weeks after Alexander's death, Nicholas realized that he would have to become Emperor and arrange for a new oath of allegiance taken to himself.

Meanwhile, in spite of the efforts to keep it all secret, rumors were flying round the capital, and the officer conspirators of the Northern Society decided to take advantage of the unrest and uncertainty to make their move. They had hoped to persuade their troops that Nicholas was a usurper, that is, that he had no right to be Emperor.

But they still could not agree on a plan of action. Some of the leaders kept changing their minds and others backed out altogether. One of them, on December 12th, went and told Nicholas there was a plot against him and then came back and told his comrades what he had done.

This meant, they felt, that it was now or never. The rising was fixed for December 14th, the day that the oath of allegiance to Nicholas was to be administered.

All the night of the 13th the insurgent leaders were going round the various barracks, trying to find out which regiments would be on their side. Nicholas by now had seen the detailed reports which had reached Alexander on his deathbed, and he too was doing all he could to find out what troops would be loyal to him. It all seemed touch and go.

At eleven in the morning the insurgent officers marched the regiments who supported them to the Senate Square. The officer they had appointed to be in command did not turn up, so all they could do was to stand in the Square, waiting for other regiments to join them.

But it turned out that a far greater number of troops were loyal to Nicholas. Before long these loyal troops were brought up and blocked all the approaches to the Square.

It was bitterly cold. Both sides stood there and waited. The Governor of Petersburg rode up and ordered the rebels to submit. But an insurgent officer shot him, and he was carried away mortally wounded.

There were further appeals to the rebels, with no effect. A few shots were exchanged. The loyalist cavalry moved out, but their horses were not properly shod, and their hoofs skidded on the slippery cobblestones.

Night comes early in the northern winter, and soon after three it was nearly dark. At four o'clock the loyalists brought up artillery. Nicholas was reluctant to give the order to fire: he did not want the beginning of his reign to be marked by bloodshed.

However, his generals insisted. A solemn warning was given to the rebels, but passed unheeded. Then the cannon opened fire. The unfortunate rebels were mown down or fled in panic. By five o'clock the insurrection was over.

When the officers of the Southern Society heard of the move in Petersburg, they decided to act themselves. But they too were uncertain and unprepared. Moreover, their natural leader had been arrested the day before the events in Petersburg.

The conspirators in the south could only muster some nine hundred troops, and after a futile little campaign across the frozen countryside, their movement too collapsed.

The authorities arrested all the officers concerned and in due course they were brought before a special tribunal. Most were deported to Siberia to serve terms of hard labor. Five were executed. Such was the end of the Decembrist Revolt.

Its leaders were men of high ideals and sincere devotion.

They failed because they were divided in their aims and methods, because they failed to organize properly, and perhaps, because Russia was not yet ripe for a movement such as theirs. But they had tried to strike a blow for liberty, and their names were honored by revolutionaries of later generations.

For many years after the Decembrist Revolt there were no plots to use armed force against the government, but this does not mean that there was no more discontent or unrest. There were a number of men of education and position (the conscience-stricken gentry) who bitterly resented the hardships suffered by the poor and their own impotence to do anything to make the régime improve their lot.

They were influenced by what was going on in France, and by the new ideas in books by Western writers. Many of these books were forbidden by the Russian censor, but they were smuggled in, passed secretly from hand to hand, and discussed in eager little private circles.

Of course the secret police were busy; there were arrests and deportations. Dostoevsky, the famous writer, was, as a very young man, a member of one of these circles. He was arrested with twenty others, condemned to death and marched out to a public square where a scaffold had been erected. Only at the last minute was the party informed that their sentences were commuted to imprisonment. Later, one of Dostoevsky's best-known books, *The House of the Dead,* was based on his prison experiences in Siberia.

Some oppositionists found they could no longer bear to live in Russia and went to live abroad, where they could read and discuss and plan and write in freedom. These *émigrés,* as they were called, came to play an important part in the Russian revolutionary movement. Two of the earlier ones, Herzen and Bakunin, though their ideas were very different, exerted great influence by their writings, which were smuggled into Russia.

Of course it was only a few of the oppositionists who emigrated. Those who stayed in Russia did what they could to develop and spread their ideas while keeping out of the clutches of the secret police. Some writers managed to deceive the censor by pretending to write on literary or philosophical themes, with a hidden political meaning for those who could understand.

As we saw in the last chapter, discontent became more widespread with the defeats and muddles of the Crimean War, and the changes brought about by Alexander II were not enough to satisfy the more ardent reformers. During the sixties and the seventies the Russian revolutionary movement attracted more and more sympathizers.

It was not a single or organized movement. The secret police were able to suppress the early attempts to form organized underground groups. And those who disliked the Czar autocracy could not agree among themselves as to how to get rid of it or what sort of government should take its place.

Some wanted to follow the example of Western Europe, some hoped to evolve a purely Russian form of Socialism. Some hoped to gain their end by peaceful means; some were certain they must use force. Some looked to a long period of plotting and conspiracy; some expected the peasants would start a revolt on their own, without any preparations made for it. And some believed that the Russian people were far too ignorant and too backward for any big change, and that the only thing to do was to get on with the work of education.

By the sixties the movement was no longer composed solely of conscience-stricken gentry. For some years to come the revolutionaries were mostly very young people, university students or ex-students or would-be students. Some were sons and daughters of gentry — mostly the poorer gentry — but many came from humble homes.

They were nearly all very poor and all were desperately in earnest. They would meet in little groups in their garrets in the big university towns and would argue night after night about the new social and political theories. They were convinced that their elders could and would do nothing to bring freedom and happiness to the Russian masses; it was they, the young revolutionaries, who must act.

Much of the history of Russia for the next twenty years is a series of unequal battles fought out between these little groups of young people on the one side, and the police and the officials and the whole establishment of the Russian Empire on the other.

In 1865 a hunchback student of Moscow University

named Ishutin and some of his friends formed the first revolutionary secret society. It contained an inner and even more secret cell called *Hell*, whose members pledged themselves to die fighting for the cause.

Neither the main organization nor Hell did anything much beyond talking and plotting. But one member decided to act on his own. This was one Karakozov, Ishutin's cousin, who had been dismissed from Moscow University because he could not pay the fees. He was a sickly youth, rather unbalanced in his mind, and he decided he would kill the Emperor Alexander. He bought a cheap pistol and fired it off at the Emperor in one of the public parks. He missed, and was caught and executed; and the police tracked down and arrested Ishutin and most of his former companions.

But other secret societies came into being. One was formed by a young man called Nechayev, the son of a sign-painter in the provinces, who managed to get to Petersburg University at the age of twenty-one in 1868. He was a determined revolutionary, brave and resourceful, but a thoroughgoing egoist and absolutely unscrupulous. In 1869 he spread a rumor that he had been arrested by the police: it was quite untrue, but the idea of his arrest and escape made him seem a hero to his companions.

Nechayev went off to Switzerland, where he joined up with the old revolutionary Bakunin. The two of them invented a whole series of high-sounding but quite imaginary revolutionary societies, managed to get hold of some money, and ferocious revolutionary pamphlets. In the summer of

1869 five hundred of these leaflets were seized at the Petersburg post office alone.

In the autumn Nechayev returned to Russia to organize the revolution. He had a powerful personality and recruited a number of young students. Some believed in his remarkable claims; some were just terrorized into doing what he told them. But there was one student, by name Ivanov, who did not entirely believe in Nechayev and was not prepared to take orders from him.

Nechayev could not stand this sort of opposition; one winter evening he and three of his underlings killed Ivanov in one of the University parks and pushed the dead body through a hole in the ice in a pond. A few days later the body was discovered, and police made a drive, arresting most of the members of Nechayev's organization.

He himself escaped abroad. He joined up again with Bakunin in Switzerland, and wrote more revolutionary articles. But he quarreled with Bakunin; and as the other *émigrés* learned more about his real character they no longer wished to collaborate with him. In 1872 he was arrested by the Swiss police and sent back to Russia under an extradition order; he was convicted of the murder of Ivanov and sentenced to imprisonment for life.

What came out at the trial about Nechayev's character and methods made a painful impression on the earnest and devoted young revolutionaries. For some years to come they confined themselves to forming circles for self-education and trying to give education to peasants and factory workers. Of course the police were on the watch: Many of these young people were arrested. But more and more came on to take their place.

The younger generation became seized with the desire to help the people. (Hence the name *Populism* that was given to the movement.) Early in 1874 there was spread the idea of going into the villages, living the same life as the villagers, teaching them and helping them.

And so hundreds of young people, in twos and threes, went off into the country on their self-imposed mission. It was all rather pathetic. They knew nothing about village life, and few of them could stand up to the hard physical strain of land-work. What was worse, they could make no real contact with the peasants, who were suspicious and could not make them out. A number of the young missionaries lost heart and went home. Then the police got busy, and before very long nearly a thousand of them were either held for trial or being kept under police supervision.

All the same the movement did advance the Populist cause. The imperial police were clumsy and often brutal; but they lacked the cold efficiency of the Bolshevik police fifty years later. A number of the prisoners were released, and many more escaped from their places of exile, and came back to continue illegal work. While they were in prison awaiting trial they had ample opportunity to exchange their ideas and make plans for the future.

At their trials they made long speeches explaining their aims and ideals. By the end of the seventies the revolutionaries enjoyed far more sympathy among the general public than they had before the "going to the people."

And during this time they had learned two important lessons. Firstly, they must have some form of organization; secondly, they must have simple slogans which the simple people could understand. Late in 1876 an organization called *Land and Liberty* came into being. The program was obvious from its name: The land was to be given to the peasants and the people should have full liberty to choose the government they wanted.

The Society had a center in Petersburg, and regional groups in the provinces. Its officers were whole-time professional revolutionaries living under strict discipline and paid from the Society's funds, which came as gifts from sympathizers and from the sale of literature. They had a secret press for printing their pamphlets and news sheets. They had a workshop for making false passports and identity papers. They had a security section, with a spy of their own working in the headquarters of the secret police. It was very different from the wild and amateurish efforts of Ishutin or of Nechayev.

But before long there were arguments over the old problem of whether to use violence or to work solely on education and propaganda. The Society included a *disorganizing section* whose work was to free prisoners, punish police informers and traitors and launch attacks against especially hostile officials. The disorganizers became very active. Rescues from prison were planned, and, at times, successfully carried out. Certain informers were killed.

But it was of course the attacks on officials that caused the greatest sensation. In January, 1878, a girl revolutionary shot and severely wounded the Chief of the Petersburg Police who had (contrary to the regulations) ordered a young student to be flogged. In May the Chief of Police in Kiev was killed. In August the head of the Third Division, the formidable secret police of the whole Empire, was stabbed to death in a street in broad daylight. The following February the Governor General of Kharkov was mortally wounded. And in early April another unsuccessful attempt was made to shoot the Emperor Alexander II.

The would-be assassin had applied to Land and Liberty to help him in his attempt, and there had been bitter disputes at the headquarters as to whether help might be given. These arguments continued.

The activists wished to go on with terrorism: They were beginning to feel that the assassination of the Emperor was the first step towards either sparking off a popular rising or forcing the government to grant political reforms. The *villagers* — those who wanted only education and propaganda in the villages — felt that the terrorists were endangering the existence of the whole movement. There were meetings and conferences, but in the end it was obvious that no agreement was possible. In August the Land and Liberty Society was wound up, and its funds, pamphlets, and equipment divided between the two wings.

After the split the villagers were unable to make much headway, and the more prominent of them emigrated abroad. The terrorist wing, under the name of *The People's Will,* then took the center of the revolutionary stage. It was not a large party. It never had more than five hundred members. Its hard core was the Executive Committee, numbering usually some fifteen or twenty. They were all young people. One was the son of a major general and one the daughter of a former governor of Petersburg; but most came from poor families. They kept very strictly to the rules they drew up for their lives and their work as revolutionaries. They were all absolutely devoted to the cause.

The Executive Committee condemned Alexander II to death in August, 1879. It was decided to blow up his train on his way back to Petersburg from the Crimea in the late autumn. The terrorists had some dynamite, made by their own scientific experts in their own laboratory. In order, as they hoped, to make quite sure, they decided to mine the track in two places.

One was an embankment near Alexandrovsk in south Russia. It was hard work for the little party that laid the mine: They could only work at night and the November nights were bitterly cold with incessant rain. They were terrified that the rain would turn to snow, which would mean that their footmarks would be seen by the railway guards. The other venture was more elaborate. The terrorists bought a cottage near the railway outside Moscow and dug an underground tunnel from the cellar to a point just under the track. Here again it was desperately hard work for these amateur young miners; but in the end both mines were laid and ready just in time.

On the morning of November 18th the convoy of imperial trains passed through Alexandrovsk station. The electrical apparatus to detonate the dynamite was got ready. As the Emperor's coach passed over the mine, Zhelyabov, the leader of the party, pressed down the lever. But nothing happened: the detonator failed to work and the trains rumbled on northward.

At ten o'clock on the evening of the following day they were nearing Moscow. The terrorists had information that Alexander was in the fourth coach of the second train. They let the first train pass. As the second train came into position there was a terrific explosion; the fourth coach crashed over on its sides, the two locomotives broke away and the remaining coaches were all derailed. The conspirators bolted into the night.

But the next day they learned that this attempt too had been a failure. Their information had been wrong: The Emperor after all had been in the first train. All they had done was to blow up the stores of fruit and jam being brought up from the south to the Imperial Palace at Petersburg. On November 22nd the Executive Committee issued a proclamation, declaring that they would continue their attacks against the Emperor until he renounced his power and handed over to a freely elected Constituent Assembly.

So the attacks went on. The most sensational was a single-handed attempt to blow up the Winter Palace. This was the idea of a revolutionary workman named Khalturin, who approached the Executive Committee for a supply of dynamite. He then got a job as carpenter handyman in the Palace. He lodged in a basement there with three other carpenters, and as luck would have it this basement was under a guard room which in turn was directly under the Emperor's dining room.

It was impossible for him to do any digging or excavating: There were far too many people about. The mine had to be a chest in the basement where Khalturin kept his clothes. Every day he went into the town and brought back a small supply of dynamite. By the beginning of February the chest was full. On the evening of the 5th he set a time fuse and left the building. Half an hour later there was a rumble and a crash. Eleven soldiers in the guard room were killed and fifty more wounded. But the dining room above the guard room was scarcely damaged; and in any case the Emperor himself had been delayed and was in another wing of the Palace at the time.

The Executive Committee went on with its campaign. There were plans for an attack on the Emperor in Odessa; but Alexander's visit to Odessa was postponed. Another scheme that went wrong was to mine one of the bridges in Petersburg. Meanwhile there were two developments that influenced the future course of events. After the explosion in the Winter Palace the Emperor appointed a Special Commission with wide powers under a very able man, Count

Loris-Melikov. Loris-Melikov set himself to smash the terrorist organization but also to introduce a number of liberal reforms so as to win back public opinion to the side of the government.

The other event was the arrest in a railway station of a young revolutionary with two large suitcases of the Executive Committee's dynamite. The youth was interrogated in prison by an extremely intelligent police officer. Little by little he was induced to give — as he thought in confidence — full details of his fellow conspirators and their organization. Later on, when he realized that he had been tricked, he was overcome with remorse and hanged himself in his cell. By that time, however, the police had enough information to track down and arrest more and more members of the People's Will.

So the final attempt of the revolutionaries against the Emperor took place in what was really a desperate race against time. One after another their key men were being arrested; and the effect of Loris-Melikov's reforms was that fewer and fewer volunteers were coming in to take their place. The People's Will's other activities, propaganda to factory workers, students, and members of the army and navy, had to be suspended because everyone was needed for the attack on the Emperor.

The plan was a twofold one. Two young revolutionaries, posing as husband and wife, took a cheese shop in a street where the Emperor often passed in his carriage. Their comrades, working in relays, dug a tunnel from the cellar of the shop to the center of the street. There they laid a mine. But there was the danger that, on the day of the attempt, the Emperor might change his route and avoid that street altogether. So four young men were chosen as bomb throwers, to be armed with bombs made in the secret laboratory and to wait for Alexander's carriage at other points along the route.

Work went on feverishly, with frequent setbacks caused by the ever-increasing raids and arrests by the police. The attempt was timed for Sunday, March 1st. On the Friday before, Zhelyabov, the leader of the enterprise, was arrested, and his fiancée, a young girl called Sophia Perovskaya, took charge. On the Saturday the mine was not yet laid and the bombs were not yet ready, and all that were left of the party had to work all night to complete their preparations.

The Emperor did not go down the street where the cheese shop was. But Perovskaya, in charge of the bomb throwers, was able to get her men into position elsewhere. Two bombs were thrown. The first killed one of the Cossack guards and a butcher boy who was watching the procession. The second mortally wounded the Emperor, who died almost as soon as he could be taken back to the Palace.

The People's Will had achieved its aim; but it seemed to bring no advantage to the revolutionary cause. There was no popular outbreak. So far from being frightened into granting the freedom of speech and freedom of elections that the revolutionaries were demanding, the new Emperor dismissed Loris-Melikov and canceled the reforms Loris-Melikov was proposing.

The police intensified their campaign against the People's Will. Sophia Perovskaya was arrested. She, Zhelyabov and three of the others were hanged in a Petersburg square in early April. By that time only eight members of the Executive Committee were left, and the arrests were still continuing. The party had been almost wiped out. Six years later a little group of students of Petersburg University tried to carry on the name and the work of the People's Will by organizing an attempt to kill Alexander III, but they were all arrested. This phase of the Russian revolutionary movement had come to an end.

For nearly twenty years after the murder of Alexander II there was what seemed to be a lull in revolutionary action in Russia. But a good deal was happening that was to affect the future of Russia and indeed of the whole world.

For one thing there was Marx. Karl Marx was born in Trier, Germany, in 1818 of a Jewish father and a German mother. As a very young man he got into trouble with the German authorities because of his revolutionary ideas. He moved to Paris in 1843; and from 1849 to his death in 1883 he spent most of his time in London, studying in the British Museum Reading Room and writing his books.

For the last few years of his life he had an allowance from his friend Engels, but most of his time he was miserably poor, living with his family in a squalid little flat in Soho and later on in Highgate.

His health was not good. He suffered from boils, which made him irritable. He was dictatorial, argumentative and quarrelsome. But he had a first-class brain and was a tremendous worker, convinced that the ideas that he was working out were of supreme importance for the future of mankind. And indeed his writings and those of his friend Engels have come to be regarded as a sort of bible by the rulers and many of the ruled in Russia, China and all the other Communist countries.

There is a note on Marx's ideas or *Marxism* at the end of the book. Perhaps it is enough to say here that Marx was convinced that in every age and in every country there was a ruling class, and that this class was made up of those who owned the means of producing what people required for their material needs.

In other words, he believed that the ruling class, in the nineteenth century, were the people who owned the factories that turned out or processed the clothes and the food and the furniture and the tools and everything else that we all require in order to live. This class he called the capitalist class or the bourgeoisie.

He further believed that this class was only concerned with its own interests, and had no regard for the welfare of other people. He found it inevitable that the factory owners should exploit their workers by getting as much labor out of them as they could for the lowest possible wages. He believed that, as industry developed, the rich would get richer and richer and the poor would get poorer and poorer.

He felt that things would get worse and worse, until one day the workers or proletariat (i.e. people who have nothing but what they can earn by manual labor) would bring about a revolution, drive out the capitalists, and themselves take over the means of production. This would mean that the factories and mines and everything else would belong to the people as a whole, and they would be worked not for the profit of a few but for the benefit of the entire community. There would be no more classes (because the capitalists would have been driven out). There would be no more exploitation of man by man. All would live happily in a Communist society.

In 1848 Marx and Engels issued a manifesto in which they wrote, "Workers of the world, unite — you have nothing to lose but your chains." They felt it the duty of all right-thinking people to assist and to hasten on the proletarian revolution.

Marx's writings began to be translated into Russian in the seventies, and thereafter more and more Russians came to be influenced by them. At that time the conditions in which the workers in Western Europe lived were bad enough, but the Russian workers were even worse off. They were miserably housed, and their wages were hardly enough to feed their families. It was felt that to be a Marxist was to be a champion of the workers.

And then Marx had worked out a whole philosophy to

explain the course of history, and this made a great appeal to the intellectuals, that is, to those educated people who were interested in such matters.

After the People's Will had been crushed, the revolutionary movement in Russia in the eighties and early nineties consisted of a number of little underground groups or circles. Some of them, the Populists, looked to the peasants to bring about a revolution. The others, the Marxists, looked to the increasing number of factory workers.

There was a good deal of argument between the leaders of these groups (especially among the *émigrés* abroad), but in Russia for the most part their relations were friendly. The Populists read and admired Marx; and it was felt that both sides were working for the cause of revolution, although along different lines.

Both Marxists and Populists had to work in secret, because the police were after them all the time. But at the turn of the century they managed to start, underground, what came to be the two great revolutionary parties — the Social Democrats (Marxists), and the Socialist Revolutionaries or SRs (Populists).

The early Marxists had some difficulty in applying Marxist ideas to Russian conditions. Marx in his writings had in mind the countries of Western Europe, where the capitalists and bourgeoisie were numerous and powerful and where there were a great many workers.

In Russia, at that time, there were only a few private factory owners. The great enemy of the revolutionary movement was the Emperor and his army officials. And the factory workers were still far too few to carry through a revolution by themselves.

Some of the early Marxists felt that all they could do was to spread Marxist ideas: Before they could act they would have to wait till the Russian workers were far more numerous and far better organized.

But just to wait was not enough for the remarkable man who later was destined to carry through the revolution. Vladimir Ilich Lenin (whose real name was Ulyanov) was the son of a senior school inspector. His mother was German. He was very young when he first became a revolutionary: His elder brother was hanged for his part in the attempt on the Emperor in 1887, and this made a great impression on him.

That same year Lenin himself was expelled from Kazan University. From 1893 to 1895 he was living in Petersburg, one of the leaders of the most active of the Marxist groups there. At the end of 1895 he was arrested, spent fourteen months in prison and was sent off to exile in Eastern Siberia. He wrote a book on economics, kept fit by going on shooting expeditions after ducks and geese, and while in exile married a girl who had been a member of his group in the capital.

It was a happy marriage, and Krupskaya, as his wife was called, was an active and very efficient partner in all his revolutionary work. In 1900 he was allowed back to Russia again, but after a few months he went abroad to contact the

Marxist *émigrés* in Switzerland. Apart from a spell in Finland (1950 to 1907) he remained abroad, mostly in England and Switzerland, until the spring of 1917.

Lenin was one of the most remarkable men of his age. Personally, he was simple, unaffected and easily approachable. In his years of exile he was always ready to help with the housework: though Krupskaya found he got so absorbed in his reading that he was apt to let the milk boil over. But as a revolutionary leader he had enormous energy and enormous force of character.

He was absolutely devoted to the revolutionary cause and absolutely confident that his own view of Marxist doctrine and of the Marxist course of action was correct. So sure was he that he was right and that people who disagreed with him were wrong, that he was quite unscrupulous in dealing with them. To Lenin any degree of force or fraud was permissible if it helped his cause. This ruthlessness in thought and action has been a mark of the Communist leaders ever since.

Lenin had very definite ideas about how the revolution could and should be brought about. Marxist theory, as we have seen, was that the proletariat (the workers) should rise, drive out the landlords and the ruling class and then establish a new order of society on Communist lines.

But Lenin found that the workers were not really interested in all this. What the workers wanted was better wages, better housing, more leisure and better conditions of life. Once they got these they would not bother about starting a revolution.

Lenin accordingly decided that he must build up a party which could act, as he put it, as the "vanguard" of the working class. The task of the party was to encourage and guide and prod the workers into revolution; to seize power in the name of the workers; and then, again in the name of the workers, establish a new order of society on Communist lines.

From the time he went abroad Lenin worked unceasingly and with great energy in building up this party. It consisted entirely of professional revolutionaries, that is, people who devoted their whole time to revolutionary work and received a small salary from revolutionary funds. Lenin saw to it that they were strictly disciplined and entirely under his orders.

In 1903 the Russian Marxists (who then called themselves the Russian Social Democratic Workers' Party) decided to hold a Congress abroad (out of reach of the Russian police) to work out a program and form of organization. Delegates were appointed and smuggled out of Russia with false passports. They assembled in Brussels, but got into trouble with the Belgian police and so moved on to London, where the police were more tolerant. There was a great deal of argument between the various groups, and the result of the Congress was that instead of one united Marxist party there came to be two — Lenin's party, the Bolsheviks (which means majority), and the Mensheviks (which means minority).[1]

[1] Lenin's Party took the name of Russian Social Democratic Workers Party (Bolshevik); in 1918, after they had seized power in Russia they changed the name to Russian Communist Party (Bolshevik).

For many years to come there were quarrels between these two parties, and for much of the time the Bolsheviks, in spite of their name, were really in the minority. The Bolsheviks had the advantage of Lenin's strong personality and outstanding intellect, and the discipline he was able to enforce on his followers. Furthermore the Mensheviks would not believe there could be really serious differences between Marxists: so that they did not fight nearly so ruthlessly against Lenin as Lenin fought against them.

On the other hand some of the Mensheviks and even some of the Bolsheviks thought Lenin too much of a dictator; they thought that in a revolutionary party the rank and file should have some say in how things were run, and they did not like Lenin's insistence on absolute obedience to the Center (which of course meant Lenin himself).

Trotsky, who at that time was neither a Bolshevik nor a Menshevik, talked about the danger of overthrowing the tyranny of the Czar only to establish a tyranny of the Party Center under Lenin.

It was also felt that Lenin did not show good faith in his dealings with other revolutionary groups and that he was unscrupulous about money matters. Lenin never wanted money for himself, of course — but he was always in urgent need of funds to finance his organization. He once got two attractive young Bolsheviks to make love to two simple-minded heiresses, and so came into possession of their fortunes.

And then Lenin encouraged what were known as *expro-*

priations, raids by armed gangs on State banks to get money for revolutionary work. Nearly all Russian revolutionaries had always had strict ideas about behavior. The SRs (but not the Bolsheviks or Mensheviks) regarded terrorist attacks on the Emperor and high officials as a proper way to fight for the revolution. But nobody approved of raising funds by criminal means, and feeling over the expropriations was such that Lenin had to give way.

There were repeated moves to try to unite the Bolsheviks and Mensheviks, but they had no lasting result. The *émigré* leaders, Lenin especially, were working hard the whole time to get control, for their own faction, of the revolutionary groups within Russia. And quite a number of the Social Democrats in Russia, with all their own local problems and the police hard after them, heartily wished that the leaders abroad would stop quarreling and let them all work together for the cause.

As we saw in the last chapter, the 1905 Revolution was quite unprepared and took the main revolutionary parties by surprise. The only well-known revolutionary to take a prominent part in it was Trotsky, and he was then neither a Bolshevik nor a Menshevik. (He was arrested when the authorities regained control and sent off to Siberia; but he soon escaped and returned to Europe.)

We have seen, too, that the years after 1906 marked a decline in the revolutionary movement, because of the hope of achieving reforms by peaceful and unrevolutionary means. It is true this was a time of great industrial development.

More and more factories were put up and more and more peasants came in from the villages to become factory workers. There were a number of quite important strikes. But insofar as the workers supported any political party the greater number of them supported the Mensheviks.

Then World War I broke out, and provoked the upsurge of patriotic feeling. Peasants and workers alike rallied to defend the Russian Motherland against the Imperialist German attack. Very few wished to listen to Lenin, then in Switzerland with a tiny band of followers, who declared that Russia should be defeated because a Russian defeat would open up the path to revolution.

The emperor with snow shovel and children on his estate shortly before the February revolution. With him are, left to right, the Czarevitch, heir to the throne, Tatiana, one of his daughters, and their cousin, Prince Nikita.

CHAPTER III

The February Revolution and the Abdication of the Emperor

When war broke out in the late summer of 1914 everyone in Russia was hoping for an early victory, but when the war dragged on and on and the Russian armies suffered serious defeats, patriotic enthusiasm began to fade. The year 1915 was a very difficult one. The troops at the front were short of arms and ammunition.

In 1916 supply services were reorganized, and cargoes of munitions were being shipped by the Western Allies to north Russian ports. The Russian armies at the front were in better shape. The Emperor Nicholas had now made himself Commander in Chief and spent most of his time at Supreme Headquarters at Mogilev in northwest Russia, where he had a capable general to act as his Chief of Staff. But all this time discontent was growing. There was especially bitter feeling against the Empress. She was of course German by birth, and rumors went round that she was working for the Germans against Russia.

These stories were quite untrue, but people believed them. What was true, however, was that the Empress was entirely under the influence of the disreputable Rasputin, and on Rasputin's advice was pressing the Emperor to appoint corrupt and incompetent men to the most important posts in the government.

There were bitter attacks in the Duma on the way these ministers were running the war. In private there were all sorts of schemes and plots. Among the liberal leaders in the Duma and their friends outside, the idea was that the Emperor must be made to resign or abdicate in favor of the little Czarevitch, with one of the easy-going Grand Dukes to act as Regent: This would mean that the real power would be in the hands of a government made up of the liberal Duma leaders.

In late December 1916 a young nobleman called Prince Yusupov (who had been at Oxford and had married the Emperor's niece) and a group of his friends decided to kill Rasputin. The plan they chose was to invite him to the richly furnished basement of Prince Yusupov's house, and give him poisoned cakes and poisoned wine. This they did. But Rasputin had an iron constitution, and the poison for the time had no effect.

Yusupov drew his revolver and fired. Rasputin dropped back, seemingly dead; but a few minutes later he was crawling on hands and knees after the conspirators. It was a grisly scene and they all lost their heads. Several more revolver shots were fired. Finally Rasputin lay still and they took the body and threw it over the parapet of one of the bridges across the freezing Neva.

Three days later, on January 1st, one of Rasputin's boots was washed up on the ice. Then divers went down and recovered the body. By this time it was well known who the murderers were, but in view of the excited public opinion the Emperor could do no more than have them banished to their country estates.

At the beginning of March 1917, bread-rationing was started in Petrograd and there was a run on the bakeries. There was a strike at one of the big factories. But no one expected serious trouble, and on March 7th the Emperor (who had been staying with his family at Tsarskoe Selo, his country palace and estate just outside the capital) went back to Supreme Headquarters at Mogilev. Next morning he had a telegram stating that his little son and one of the girls were down with measles.

That same day, March 8th, there were big demonstrations of working-class women and strikers. Some of them shouted slogans against the war and against the autocracy. A few bread shops were looted.

By now, in the third winter of war, the workers had got thoroughly tired of war conditions. Prices had risen sharply, but wages had not. There were long weary queues at the food shops. In Russia as a whole there was at that time

A sailor delivers a speech to soldiers of one of the Petrograd barracks, but part of his audience is more interested in the photographer.

plenty of food for everybody, but owing to transport difficulties there were often shortages in the big towns.

On March 9th there were bigger demonstrations. Ninety thousand more workers went on strike and fifty factories were closed. The cabinet ministers telegraphed asking the Emperor to come back to the capital; and the politicians in the Duma began to hope that the time had come when the Emperor would be forced to agree to a representative government with themselves in charge.

On March 10th the Emperor wired back that the disorders must be suppressed.

On that same day, in Petrograd, more workers came out. There was what amounted to a general strike. No newspapers appeared. The students left the university and joined the demonstrations in the streets.

The officer commanding the Petrograd garrison did not take very drastic steps to stop the demonstrations. He realized his troops were inclined to sympathize with the strikers. On the 11th some units did obey orders to open fire on crowds which refused to disperse, but they did so reluctantly.

On the 12th, one of the key days of the revolution, practically all of the 160,000 soldiers who formed the garrison refused to take any steps at all against the demonstrators. In fact they ignored their officers and joined the demonstrations themselves.

Vast crowds moved along the main streets, shouting revolutionary slogans. There were some attacks on unpopular police officials and Czarist ministers. The law courts were burned; and a huge crowd forced its way into the main prison, released the prisoners and set the building on fire. All this time the crowds, on the whole, were good-humored.

But nobody, neither the officials nor the politicians nor the demonstrators themselves, knew exactly what was happening and nobody was really sure what to do next. There was little leadership. The more prominent revolutionary leaders of the time were either in prison, in exile or abroad. But in the evening some of the Left Wing and labor representatives who remembered what had happened in 1905 met together in a journalist's flat and decided there should be a

Soviet of Workers' and Soldiers' Deputies; elections were held by the factory workers and the rank and file of the various regiments, and the Soviet began to hold sessions in one wing of the Tauride Palace.

This vast Palace was where the Duma sat, and in another wing there were the members of the Duma who had formed a committee and who were sending messages to urge the Emperor to empower them to form a government.

The Emperor at first ignored these messages. Nobody at the Supreme Headquarters in Mogilev (and indeed no one in Russia outside Petrograd) had any idea that the imperial authority in the capital had practically ceased to exist.

But on the 13th Nicholas decided to return to Tsarskoe Selo. He was worried about the health of the children. All five were coming down with measles, and one of the girls caught pneumonia as well. He started off in his special train that night. But then it was learned that revolutionaries were blocking the line, and the train had to be diverted. The next evening it had got to Pskov.

During the twenty-four hours that the train remained on the siding at Pskov the whole history of Russia was changed. There were unceasing telegrams between Pskov and Petrograd. The Emperor's Chief of Staff telegraphed round to the leading generals to find out what they thought should be done. Two representatives of the Duma liberals arrived from Petrograd on an urgent mission to persuade the Emperor to abdicate.

The replies from the senior generals showed they nearly

all thought that the Emperor should appoint a responsible government and then abdicate in favor of his son. Of course neither they, nor the Emperor himself, knew how far things had gone in the capital. They imagined the Duma leaders were in full control there. Nicholas was still in his train on a siding in Pskov railway station. When he heard the views of all his generals, he decided to give way. At first he appointed his son to succeed him, as everybody was advising. Then he had a talk with the family doctor, and when the latter assured him that the boy's illness was incurable he decided instead to appoint his own brother, Michael. He signed the act of abdication at midnight.

Next day the news was brought to the Grand Duke Michael in Petrograd. But he had seen what had been happening, and felt that to be Emperor was far too difficult and risky a business. So he too abdicatd. And so after many centuries of autocratic rule Russia found herself without a Czar.

The ex-Emperor Nicholas went back in his train from Pskov to Mogilev, where he handed over his command and said good-bye to his officers and troops. Here he was told he was under arrest, and went back under escort to join his family at Tsarkoe Selo. His idea was to stay there until the family were well again.

His cousin, King George V, invited the whole family to come and stay in England. Plans were made for them to go by train to Port Romanov on the extreme northern tip of

Russia, where a British warship would come and take them on board. But when these plans leaked out there was an outcry by the extremists of the Petrograd Soviet, who insisted that the imperial family should be kept under arrest in Russia. So they remained, under guard, in a wing of the Tsarskoe Selo Palace, until the late summer, when the Provisional Government sent them to Tobolsk in Siberia.

CHAPTER IV

The Provisional Government and
the Petrograd Soviet

While the negotiations were going on in the Emperor's train at Pskov the crowds were marching up and down the streets of Petrograd giving cheers for the revolution; and the two new groups which had emerged were watching each other with some suspicion.

One was the Soviet of Workers and Soldiers, which had at its head an Executive Committee composed mostly of those who had met in the journalist's flat. The other was the Committee of the Duma politicians. Both these groups had one fear in common — that monarchist officers would bring in troops and restore the autocracy. There was in fact no real danger of this, but both parties thought that there was.

But in addition the Soviet was afraid that the Duma Committee would use troops to suppress the Soviet, and the Duma Committee thought the Soviet was working for mob rule and anarchy.

To ward off the supposed danger from the army, during the night of March 14th-15th some members of the Soviet drew up an Order No. 1 addressed to the Petrograd garrison. This laid down, among other things, that all military and naval units should elect committees of the rank and file, which would be under the orders of the Soviet; these committees were to take charge of all arms and ammunition, and not let the officers have any control of them.

This Order No. 1 was widely published in the press and though it was addressed only to the Petrograd garrison, army units all over the country and at the front began to elect committees. The feeling spread among the soldiers that there was no longer any need to bother about what the officers told them, and discipline through the whole army began to decline.

Meanwhile, after a lot of hard bargaining, an agreement between the Soviet and the Duma Committee was reached during the night of March 15th. By this the Soviet agreed that, for the time being, a Provisional Government as suggested by the Duma should be the government of Russia. This government was made up of men of liberal views who were Duma members or had worked on war committees and local government councils.

(The Soviet representatives turned down a suggestion that members of the Soviet should take posts in the government. They did not want the Soviet to be held responsible for anything that the Provisional Government did. But one of their members, a Socialist lawyer, Kerensky, very much wanted to be a minister, and in a dramatic speech he persuaded the Soviet to let him become Minister of Justice.)

It was also agreed between the Soviet and the Duma that there should be absolute freedom of speech and of the press. All political prisoners and exiles were to be freed. All local authorities were to be freely elected. The old police force was abolished. And the units of the Petrograd garrison — which had played so large a part in bringing about the revolution — were not to be disarmed and not sent away from the capital.

As to the future, it was agreed that everybody in the country should vote for delegates to a kind of super-parliament — Constituent Assembly was the name given to it — and this body should decide exactly how the new free Russia should be ruled. As there had never been free elections in Russia before, it would naturally take weeks and months before arrangements for this general election could be made.

It was all rather vague. There was nothing in it about war aims, or on what terms Russia would be prepared to make peace. And what the peasants all over the country wanted was to be given the landlords' land; and there was nothing about that in the agreement either.

And it was a half-hearted agreement. The Soviet was determined only to support the Provisional Government if it did as the Soviet wanted; and it was often hard to say exactly what the Soviet did want. It was made up mostly of simple-minded and often muddle-headed men who wanted to go on with the revolution until everybody, as they hoped, would be free and happy and prosperous. But they had too little experience of practical politics to have clear ideas how to bring this about.

As for the Provisional Government, it too was mostly made up of men who had little experience of governing. They did not want to make any big decisions, because these they felt should be taken by the Constituent Assembly when it was elected. They were rather afraid of the Soviet, and anyhow if they did give any orders they could not be sure they would be carried out because the old police force had been abolished and because they had no real control over the Petrograd garrison.

But in the country as a whole, for these first few weeks, the general mood was one of great enthusiasm and optimism. It was realized that there was still a great deal to be done. But at least, after centuries of autocracy, the old despotism had been swept away and Russia, it seemed, was at last a free country.

All this time Lenin, as we have seen, had been living quietly in exile in Switzerland. Like everybody else he had been surprised at the events of March. Only a few weeks before, he had been doubting whether a revolution in Russia would take place in his lifetime. But as soon as he heard the news he was burningly impatient to get back to Russia and lead his Bolshevik Party.

The problem was how to get there, across the fighting

line of the huge Eastern front. But within a few weeks the solution was provided by the Germans.

Throughout the war the Germans had been looking for every possible means to weaken their Russian enemy. One way was to encourage the revolution. If a revolution upset the Russian Government it would lead to the disorganization of the Russian Army. So the Germans discreetly supported the Russian revolutionary leaders abroad, supplied them with funds and helped them to smuggle their propaganda into Russia. (Soviet historians indignantly deny that the Bolsheviks ever received money from the Germans, but there are documents to prove that they did.)

After the March revolution the Germans were more than ever eager to knock Russia out of the war altogether; and as Lenin wanted Russia to stop the war at once, the Germans felt it to their advantage that he should go back to Russia, where he could make his influence felt.

There were very secret negotiations, and it was arranged that a party of revolutionaries, including Lenin, should embark in early April on a "sealed train" in Switzerland and be carried all through Germany to a port on the Baltic, where they could take the ferry to Sweden. Sweden being a neutral country, it would then be quite easy for them to make their way on to Russia.

The Germans had no intention of letting loose any revolutionaries in Germany (who might make trouble for the German Government) and so the train was sealed; nobody

Lenin addresses a street meeting in the spring of 1918. Trotsky, in uniform, is to the lower right of Lenin's platform.

could get in or out all the way between the Swiss frontier and the Swedish ferry.

The party set off on April 9th. There were thirty-two of them, including nineteen Bolsheviks. Not all revolutionaries are punctual and one of them missed the train, though he had sent his luggage on board. He himself was of little importance, but his luggage caused a lot of worry to the German railway officials, who thought that a revolutionary's luggage might easily contain a bomb.

Lenin arrived in Petrograd on April 16th and started to put forward his views with such vehemence that even his Petrograd Bolshevik supporters were astonished. These Petrograd Bolsheviks had hitherto imagined they were doing their revolutionary duty by taking part in the Petrograd Soviet. Lenin would have none of this. He said the Soviet was merely helping the Provisional Government. He maintained that the Provisional Government should be swept away and that the Soviet should seize power in the name of the proletariat.

Lenin maintained that what was left of the old order must be abolished. The landowners and factory owners must be disposessed. The war must be stopped at once, and the Russian soldiers at the front should fraternize with the German soldiers in the opposite trenches so as to hurry on a revolution in Germany as well.

These ideas had a mixed reception. Even serious-minded Bolsheviks thought this was going too fast. Their view of Marxist theory was that there should be a long period of liberal democratic government before the proletariat could seize power. And thinking people of the other parties, even of the revolutionary parties, were against peace at any price because they thought their Russian Revolution must be defended against the attacks of imperial Germany.

But before long simple workers in the factories and peasants in the villages seemed to be favoring Lenin's proposals. They were tired of the war and they wanted the land and they were not really interested in anything else.

In a very few weeks the Bolshevik Party as a whole agreed that Lenin's tactics were correct. The Party began to show great activity, calling for peace at the front, for the splitting up of landlords' property among the peasants in the villages, and for the overthrow of the "bourgeois and capitalist" Provisional Government.

In May there were street demonstrations against the Provisional Government, as a result of which the government was reorganized to include six Socialist ministers. Kerensky, whom we have already mentioned, now became Minister of War.

Kerensky was a sincere Socialist with a strong sense of the dramatic. He saw himself as chosen to play the part of the leader of the new Russia. He was a tremendous orator, capable of stirring huge audiences with his dramatic and emotional speeches. The trouble was, of course, that the effect of his speeches on the crowds would soon wear off and the basic Russian problems still remained unsolved.

It was Kerensky who was largely responsible for the decision that the Russian Army should launch an offensive against the Germans and Austrians. He was inspired by what he had read of the French Revolution, when the French revolutionary armies had conquered in the name of Liberty, Equality, Faternity. He felt, too, that big victory would restore the morale of the Russian troops and would rally the Russian people as a whole in support of the Provisional Government.

Also the British and French were pressing for a Russian offensive which would prevent the Germans transferring more troops to the front in France; and there were a great many Russians (including some Socialists) who felt that Russia must keep faith with her Western allies.

Kerensky himself went round the front, making resounding speeches to the soldiers. And on July 1st the attack was launched. At first it seemed that it would be successful. The Austrian troops gave ground. Then the Germans counterattacked and the Russian advance was halted. Soon the Russians had to retreat, and in a few days' time the retreat became a rout.

In the middle of the month there was serious trouble in Petrograd. On the 16th there were strikes and demonstrations and shouts of "Down with the Government" and "All power to the Soviets." Next day several thousand revolutionary sailors arrived from the naval base of Kronstadt.

Demonstrations in Petrograd became more violent and there were a number of clashes. Chernov, one of the leaders of the Socialist Revolutionary Party, was seized by the mob and might have been lynched but for Trotsky, who told the crowd to let him go. For a time it seemed touch and go whether or not the Provisional Government would be swept away by the crowds of sailors and soldiers and armed factory workers — whose leaders would inevitably be the Bolshevik Party.

And then the tide turned. It seemed that most of the army units did not, as yet, wish to sweep away the Provisional Government. They kept the crowds away from the Tauride Palace where the Cabinet was sitting. The workers got tired of demonstrating and went home.

The Provisional Government — once more in control of the capital — issued documents tending to show that Lenin and the Bolshevik Party had been receiving money from the Germans, and issued a warrant for the arrest of Lenin and others. All this had an enormous effect. Even the crowds who had been shouting "Down with the Government" now turned their anger against the Bolsheviks.

The Bolsheviks of course indignantly denied the accusations. But it is interesting to note that Lenin was unwilling to stand his trial and face the charges in open court. Instead he disguised himself, shaved off his beard, and went into hiding.

It seemed dangerous to remain in the Petrograd area, so he got an engineer to take him on his locomotive (pretending to be the fireman) to Finland, where he hid in the house of a friend and settled down to write another book.

CHAPTER V

The Kornilov Affair

After the July Days there were more Cabinet reshuffles, and Kerensky became Prime Minister. Now, at last, the bulk of public opinion was behind the Provisional Government; there seemed the chance that it could really start to govern Russia.

But very little happened apart from speech-making. Nothing was done about giving land to the peasants, and the peasants grew more and more restive. And, oddly, little was done to suppress the main internal enemy of the Provisional Government — that is to say, the Bolshevik Party.

Trotsky (who had now joined the Bolsheviks) and a few others were arrested. But nobody was brought to trial. Gradually the Bolsheviks were able to go on with their work of propaganda and organization. They were particularly active in their work in the army — their object being to destroy army discipline so that army units could never be used against them.

They were also building up an armed force of their own — the Red Guards. These were made up of pro-Bolshevik factory workers. It was easy to get rifles for them from pro-Bolshevik soldiers.

It was the army that was now the main concern of Kerensky and his government. After the crushing defeat of the July offensive, the army was in a bad way. Discipline had gone to pieces. Large numbers of soldiers were deserting and streaming back to home to their villages. The supply services were becoming chaotic.

Kerensky realized that to get things under control he must appoint as Commander in Chief a general with a really strong character. His choice was General Kornilov, and there were confidential negotiations between Kornilov and Kerensky as to the steps which ought to be taken.

While these negotiations were going on Kerensky called a State Conference in Moscow for the end of August — the object being to get nationwide support for himself and his policy.

It was a huge conference — 2,500 delegates representing the Soviets, the Duma, the army, the trade unions, the employers, in fact all sections of Russian life. Only the Bolsheviks did not attend; but they instigated a general strike in Moscow, so that many of the delegates could not find cabs to take them to the conference.

The conference only showed that unity was impossible.

One half of those present wanted more discipline; the other half wanted more freedom. Each side abused the other, and there was little sign of that whole-hearted confidence it had been hoped the conference would produce.

At the end of the proceedings Kerensky made a very long dramatic speech — which left him dazed and exhausted — appealing for unity. But it was just another speech.

Meanwhile the confidential Kerensky-Kornilov negotiations were going on. The emotional Socialist statesman and the tough hard-bitten general were very unlike in temperament. Kornilov came from a poor Siberian Cossack family; he had made his way to the top entirely by his own efforts. As a young officer he had made a number of adventurous journeys into Central Asia: He knew several of the native languages. In 1915 he had been taken prisoner when his headquarters was overrun by the Austrians. But he escaped and got back to Russia, where he proved himself a first-rate fighting general.

Kornilov was no monarchist. He had no wish to see the autocracy restored. But he was a sincere patriot. He wanted Russia to win the war, and he saw no chance of that unless discipline and order were established not only in the army at the front but in the rear areas as well.

In late August it seemed that agreement in principle had been reached between Kerensky and Kornilov as to the steps to be taken. These included the reintroduction of the death penalty for serious offenses, not only at the front, but also in the garrisons in the interior, the reorganization of the rear areas so as to ensure supplies for the army, and the dispatch of a special task force to Petrograd.

This last was especially important. The new measures were likely to provoke angry demonstrations, perhaps even a Bolshevik-led rising against the Provisional Government; and no reliance could be placed on the Petrograd garrison to come out in their defense.

There was never much mutual trust between Kerensky (who thought Kornilov a reactionary) and Kornilov (who thought Kerensky a revolutionary demagogue). Nevertheless the preparations went on and it was only at the last minute that the break came.

This was in great part due to the antics of a busybody called V. N. Lvov, who went to see Kornilov at Supreme Headquarters in Mogilev, making out he was Kerensky's representative, and then came back to Kerensky in Petrograd to tell him what he believed Kornilov was intending to do.

Kerensky at once became suspicious and called up Kornilov at Supreme Headquarters on the direct line, pretending to be Lvov.

(In those days in Russia long-distance telephones were unreliable, so people used what they called the direct telegraph line. This was a sort of teleprinter. One speaker stood by the operator, who tapped out the message, and when the speaker at the other end had read it he gave his answer in the same way.)

It was of course quite absurd that a Prime Minister

should pretend to be somebody else when addressing his own Commander in Chief. But anyhow Kerensky thought that this telegraph conversation confirmed his worst suspicions and that Kornilov intended to arrest him and the members of his government and set up a military dictatorship.

He at once issued an order dismissing Kornilov. Kornilov refused to accept it. Kerensky forbade the dispatch of the task force to Petrograd. Kornilov sent it on its way. Some of Kerensky's government friends tried (in vain) to induce him to seek a compromise. Both sides started issuing proclamations which got more and more vehement and violent.

Then the Petrograd Soviet took a hand. The Soviet as a whole and indeed all the Left Wingers were afraid (with some justification) of what General Kornilov might do if he ever came to power, and were determined to do their utmost to oppose him.

They called on the Bolsheviks to join them, and set up a Committee for the Struggle against Counter-Revolution on which the Bolsheviks were represented. The Bolsheviks were very ready to join in. As Lenin (still in hiding) said: "We will not fight on behalf of Kerensky but we will fight against Kornilov."

The Committee sent out resounding appeals to the workers and soldiers to unite to save the revolution. Arms were issued to the workers, and over twenty thousand volunteers came in to join the Bolshevik Red Guards. Railwaymen tore up the lines on the western approaches to

Petrograd to prevent the arrival of the task force, and revolutionary speakers hurried out to meet it and harangue the rank and file.

The soldiers of the task force were bewildered. Some of them deserted. Their commanding general came on into Petrograd and shot himself. In the rest of the army the top generals were on the side of Kornilov, but there was nothing they could do, because the rank and file were under the influence of the regimental committees and the regimental committees were under the influence of the Soviet.

By September 12th the Kornilov movement had collapsed. On the 13th Kornilov himself and some of his leading generals were placed under arrest on Kerensky's orders.

The Kornilov Affair had caused enormous excitement but little bloodshed. At Viborg in Finland ten pro-Bolshevik officers had been thrown into the harbor and drowned. Four naval officers on one of the battleships were shot by the sailors. But otherwise there were very few casualties.

Kerensky and his Cabinet were still, officially, in power, But there had been a striking change in the mood throughout the country. The Bolsheviks could now claim to have been the leaders in the "victory over the counter-revolution," and their power and influence rapidly increased.

Trotsky was let out of prison and took his place in the Petrograd Soviet. On September 13th the Soviet, for the first time, showed a majority for a resolution proposed by the Bolsheviks. A few days later the Moscow Soviet did the same. In Petrograd the Bolsheviks had now many thousands of well-armed Red Guards, and when the authorities asked for the rifles to be returned to the Government arsenals the Red Guards refused to give them up. Throughout Russia more and more Bolsheviks and pro-Bolsheviks were being returned in elections to committees and congresses.

The mood was changing too among the Right Wingers and middle-of-the-roaders and all those who wished to see discipline restored in the army and law and order in the towns and the countryside. They had once hoped that the Provisional Government could bring this about, but now they no longer had any confidence in Kerensky.

In the army Bolshevik propaganda was intensified. Discipline got worse. More and more soldiers deserted and went home, some of them taking their rifles with them. If the Germans had attacked they could have made huge advances at little cost. But they preferred to keep their troops for the coming battles in the west. Russia, they felt, was beaten anyhow.

In the factories there were strikes and squabbles and shortages of raw materials. There was plenty of food still in Russia, but transport was working so badly that in some places food was short. Peasants started attacking the houses of the country landlords, stealing firewood and burning their grain and hay. As we have seen, the old police force had been abolished and no efficient new police force had been devised. The last few months of the Provisional Government was a wonderful time for thieves and bandits.

Kerensky several times reshuffled his government. He called together conferences and congresses. There was end-less speech-making. Perhaps the Provisional Government might have regained authority and influence if it had taken decisions to stop the unpopular war and divide up the land among the peasants.

But it was felt that such important decisions must be left to the Constituent Assembly, and preparations for the elections to this assembly had still not been completed.

Lenin, in his hiding-place in Finland, was of course eagerly watching how events were shaping. Very soon after the Kornilov affair he was writing vehement letters to the Bolshevik Party Central Committee in Petrograd, urging them to prepare at once to seize power by force.

Most of the other top Bolsheviks thought that Lenin was being too impatient. Things, they felt, were moving their way as it was. In early October, Trotsky was elected Chairman of the Petrograd Soviet, and the new Presidium (a sort of managing committee of the Soviet, working under the Chairman) had a Bolshevik majority.

The Bolsheviks were also gaining control of the Moscow Soviet and the Soviets of the other big cities. A Congress of all Soviets was due to take place in early November. The Party leaders were hoping for a Bolshevik majority at this Congress: They felt that once they had a majority, that would be the time for taking over power. But Lenin was not satisfied with this.

On October 22nd the Petrograd Soviet decided to appoint a Military Revolutionary Committee. The non-Bolshevik members of the Soviet thought this would be useful in keeping close contact between the Petrograd garrison and the Soviet so as to prevent any fresh counter-revolutionary move like that of Kornilov; and perhaps also to defend Petrograd against a German attack if the Germans made a new offensive.

But the Bolsheviks saw in the committee a means of getting all the armed forces in the area under Bolshevik control. And they were clever in packing it with Party members and sympathizers so that the Committee had a pro-Bolshevik majority. Trotsky himself became its leading figure.

In the night of October 23rd there took place in Petrograd an important secret meeting of the Bolshevik Central Committee. Lenin came out of his hiding-place to attend it. He still had his beard shaved off, and also wore a wig to complete his disguise.

All through the night he argued, stormed and raged, and in the end he got his way. In the small hours a majority of the Central Committee passed a resolution that the Bolsheviks must bring about an armed rising, and that the time was now ripe.

Lenin went back into hiding. Trotsky and his Revolutionary Military Committee (or R.M.C.) pressed ahead with the preparations. One of his steps was to order an arms factory to hand over 5,000 rifles for the Party's Red Guards.

He had no legal authority to give such an order but he was now so important and the Provisional Government so weak that the rifles were handed over.

CHAPTER VI

The October Revolution and the Bolshevik Seizure of Power

There was a curious atmosphere in Petrograd at that time. Winter was coming on. It was cold, with sleet and rain, and the days had drawn in so that it was dark by four o'clock in the afternoon.

Criminals were active. There were holdups in the streets and robberies every night. For the poor it was a very hard time because prices were rocketing and there were long queues at all the food shops. But the rich seemed determined to live luxuriously; expensive restaurants, theatres and night clubs were all packed, and gambling houses were open all night.

There was a feverish excitement in the air. The city was buzzing with all sorts of rumors. It was an open secret that the Bolsheviks intended to stage an uprising. But nobody knew when. Indeed, the Bolsheviks themselves did not know when, because a lot of argument was still going on in the Party Central Committee.

The All-Russian Congress of Soviets, due to start on November 2nd, had to be postponed because only a few of the delegates had arrived in Petrograd.

The Provisional Government found it difficult to know what steps to take. One idea was to send some of the disloyal Petrograd garrison to the front (to be replaced by troops loyal to the government, if any could be found). But the units refused to move; the last thing the soldiers wanted was to go to the front and fight the Germans. The Revolutionary Military Committee announced that all orders to troops must be endorsed by the R.M.C.

A meeting of delegates from the garrison units passed a resolution that the Soviets must take over power. The R.M.C. appointed pro-Bolshevik commissars to advise and lead the various regiments.

On November 4th there were big demonstrations of workers and Red Guards through the principal streets.

On November 5th Trotsky visited the Peter and Paul Fortress in the heart of the city. The troops of this fortress (with its heavy guns and well-stocked arsenal) had shown signs of wanting to be neutral between the government and the Reds. But Trotsky won them over, and all the arms in the arsenal were made available to the Red Guards.

All that day members of the Provisional Government were deliberating in the Winter Palace, which was then their headquarters. They decided to arrest the Revolutionary Military Committee and a number of leading Bolsheviks, and to close down their newspaper. There was also the cruiser *Aurora*, anchored in the River Neva, whose crew were thought to be pro-Bolshevik, and orders were given that she should put out to sea.

The trouble was how to enforce these orders. The only troops the Government could rely on were the Junkers (the cadets at the military academies) and the Women's Battalion of Death. This last was a regiment recruited in the darkest days of the war from women and girl volunteers who had sworn to fight to the death against the Germans. They were now sent to guard the government in the Winter Palace.

On November 6th the Junkers raided the office of the Bolshevik newspaper. But no leading Bolsheviks were arrested, and the *Aurora* stayed where she was.

That same afternoon, November 6th, the Bolshevik Central Committee met to consider its final plans. From his hiding-place in the city Lenin sent a message: "It must be this evening or tonight." At midnight he appeared, still in disguise, at the Bolshevik headquarters. By that time the action had already begun.

All through the night detachments under the orders of the R.M.C. were taking possession of key points in the city — the Telephone Exchange, the Telegraph Head Office, the main bridges and railway stations, the State Bank. By the morning of the 7th the Winter Palace was more or less surrounded and most of its telephone lines had been cut.

All night the members of the Provisional Government

had been feverishly deliberating. When morning came Kerensky decided his only course was to go out and rally some loyal troops. There was an American Embassy car in the courtyard, with the Stars and Stripes on its bonnet; he got into this car and muffled up his face and so managed to get past the Red patrols.

His colleagues in the Winter Palace, with the Women's Battalion and a few Junkers got ready to defend the building until Kerensky returned with reinforcements.

By the late afternoon the Winter Palace had been completely surrounded. At 6:30 (by then of course it was quite dark) an ultimatum was sent demanding that the Palace should surrender. At nine the *Aurora* fired a round of blank. After this there was some rifle and machine-gun firing from both sides. Several windows were broken but there were very few casualties.

At this time the Petrograd City Council was in session. When the news came through, its non-Bolshevik members passed a brave resolution that they would march to the Palace and die with their lawful government. So they set out, a long procession of middle-aged gentlemen (and two or three middle-aged ladies), but as they got near, the sailors and Red Guards refused to allow them through, so they had to go back to bed.

Meanwhile the shooting went on round the Winter Palace. Then it was found that one of the doors in the rear of the building had been left unguarded; some sailors and Red Guards pushed their way in. They were followed by others, more and more, pushing and scuffling along the vast corridors of the Palace.

There was no hard fighting. In the whole of the siege of the Winter Palace only half-a-dozen people were killed and these probably by stray bullets. In the final stages, when defense was obviously hopeless, the Junkers and the women soldiers allowed themselves to be disarmed.

At two o'clock in the morning the leader of the attacking force pushed into the inner council chamber where the Cabinet Ministers were sitting and told them, in the name of the Revolutionary Military Committee, that they were under arrest. During the night of the 7th-8th November 1917, the Provisional Government had been swept away and the Bolsheviks had seized power.

The Congress of Soviets met at last on the evening of November 7th, while the fighting was still going on round the Winter Palace. The Bolsheviks together with the Left Socialist Revolutionaries (who had split away from the SR Party) had a majority. But there was a big minority made up of the Mensheviks and the other SRs who disapproved of the Bolsheviks seizing power by force.

There were heated arguments, and the anti-Bolshevik minority walked out of the Congress as a protest. This of course suited the Bolsheviks, who were now able to pass a resolution to say that the Congress had assumed supreme power in Russia.

Next evening the Congress met again. This time Lenin

dominated the proceedings and proposed and carried three important resolutions. The first was for an immediate peace with the Germans; the second was that all landlords' land should be taken away from them without compensation; and the third set up a Council of People's Commissars (all of them Bolsheviks), a sort of cabinet which was to govern Russia until the meeting of the Constituent Assembly.

It was all very well for the Bolshevik-led Congress and the Council of People's Commissars to proclaim themselves the government of Russia. It remained to be seen whether Russia would agree to be governed by them. Nearly all the newspapers of November 8th had come out strongly against the Bolshevik seizure of power, and there was obviously a lot of anti-Bolshevik feeling in the capital. Kerensky was somewhere in the country collecting troops to restore the Provisional Government.

No one knew what was likely to happen in Moscow and in the other big towns.

The non-Bolshevik Socialists were all insisting that the new government must be a free coalition of all the Socialist Parties, that is to say a government in which members of all the Socialist Parties held posts. Some of the leading Bolsheviks took the same view, so there was a split within the Bolshevik Party.

Finally the powerful railway workers' union (most of whose members were Mensheviks) threatened to go on strike unless a coalition government was formed of all the Socialist parties. A railway strike would have meant cutting

Petrograd's food supply, and would have made it difficult for the Bolsheviks to extend their control to other districts.

Lenin, of course, had no intention of accepting a free coalition. He intended Russia to be ruled by the Bolshevik Party under the Party's leadership, with himself in the saddle.

For the next few days he argued, threatened and cajoled. He made the dissident members of his Party toe the line. The talks with the railway workers were allowed to trail on for three weeks, and then the Left SRs agreed to take part in the government. This made it possible to say that there was now a coalition, and the railway workers withdrew their threat of a strike. Lenin was not afraid of the Left SRs: He knew he could get rid of them whenever he wanted to.

On the whole, things had been going Lenin's way. Kerensky was only able to collect a small force of Cossacks, and when it came to the point they were unwilling to fight. The general commanding them was taken prisoner and brought to Petrograd (where the Bolsheviks tried to persuade him to come over to their side). Kerensky disguised himself as a sailor and escaped abroad.

In Petrograd itself the Junkers and a few officers staged an uprising on November 10th and seized the Telephone Exchange. There was some sharp fighting — with many more casualties than when the Bolsheviks seized power — but after a few hours the uprising was suppressed. There was more serious fighting in Moscow which lasted for some days, but on November 15th the Bolsheviks and their supporters stormed the Kremlin and gained control of the city. Meanwhile news was coming in of further Bolshevik successes in most of the other big centers.

Of course, Lenin was leaving nothing to chance. The Military Revolutionary Committee had a number of security squads, and these, right from the beginning, went round arresting anybody they thought likely to be dangerous to the new régime.

Special attention was paid to the newspapers, most of which were anti-Bolshevik. Some were officially forbidden to appear. Others were forcibly suppressed by the security squads or their stocks of newsprint taken away so that they could not appear.

Lenin himself was convinced that if his new government was to survive it would have to make use of terror. *Terror* in this sense means catching (and normally shooting) the government's internal enemies, and thus terrorizing all who might otherwise be inclined to take action against the government.

A Special Commission or Cheka was established in December to carry out this task. It took over the work of the R.M.C. security squads, and was soon greatly extended and given wide powers.

It was rather like the old Czarist secret police, but was much more ruthless and drastic. It was hastily got together, and at first recruited a great many criminal types. Stories of their drunkenness and robberies and murders of innocent people got out abroad and shocked many who would otherwise have sympathized with the Bolshevik Revolution.

But the Cheka did terrorize, and it did kill a number of the régime's enemies. Lenin himself was satisfied that it played an essential part in enabling the Bolsheviks to maintain themselves in power.

About the time of the Bolshevik rising in Petrograd the elections to the Constituent Assembly were taking place all over Russia. These were the first and last entirely free general elections ever to be held in the country.

Most Russians were looking to the Constituent Assembly finally to settle how Russia was to be governed. All the political parties, including the Bolsheviks, had been supporting the idea of it.

But now the Bolsheviks were in power they had no intention of handing over power to an Assembly in which they might be in a minority. Lenin was adamant on this point, and began to prepare for all eventualities.

There were 707 seats in the Constitutent Assembly and when the elections were completed the anti-Bolshevik Socialist Revolutionaries secured 370 of them — an absolute majority. The Bolsheviks had 175 seats and their Left SR allies 40.

The Assembly was due to meet in the Tauride Palace in Petrograd on January 18th. There was tension and excitement in the city.

On that day, a big demonstration was arranged in support of the anti-Bolshevik SRs. Two regiments of the garrison wished to take part. But the SR headquarters told them that if they did they must not carry their arms. This disgusted the soldiers: They knew the Bolsheviks were likely to shoot, and they saw no point in demonstrating unless they could shoot back.

As it turned out the Reds did shoot, and the demonstration was dispersed.

At the Tauride Palace all the guards, of course, were under Bolshevik orders.

When the proceedings opened, the Bolsheviks proposed a resolution that the Constituent Assembly should recognize the Bolshevik Government and should, in effect, not have the power to decide how the Russia of the future was to be governed. This was, of course, rejected by a large majority, and the Bolsheviks and Left SRs withdrew from the hall.

The remaining delegates, mostly Right Wing SRs, passed a resolution on land reform and were going on with their business when the commander of the guards on duty told the chairman they must now stop, as his men were tired. The chairman tried to insist on going on, but then all the lights were turned off, and the delegates pushed out of the building.

Those that tried to come back next morning found that the doors were locked and Red Guards posted all round, That was the end of the Constituent Assembly.

CHAPTER VII

The Peace of Brest-Litovsk

As we have said, the two problems which the Provisional Government had failed to solve were peace and land. After Lenin's resolution at the Congress of Soviets on November 8th that the country landlords should be dispossessed, the peasants, all over the country, had just walked in and grabbed the land, so that the land problem, for the time being, was solved.

There remained the problem of peace. In mid-November the Bolsheviks in Moscow sent a message to General Dukhonin, Commander in Chief at Supreme Headquarters in Mogilev, telling him to arrange a cease-fire with the Germans.

But General Dukhonin had been appointed by Kerensky and did not regard the Bolsehviks as the lawful government of Russia: He thought they were a group of conspirators who had seized the capital and who, in their turn, were

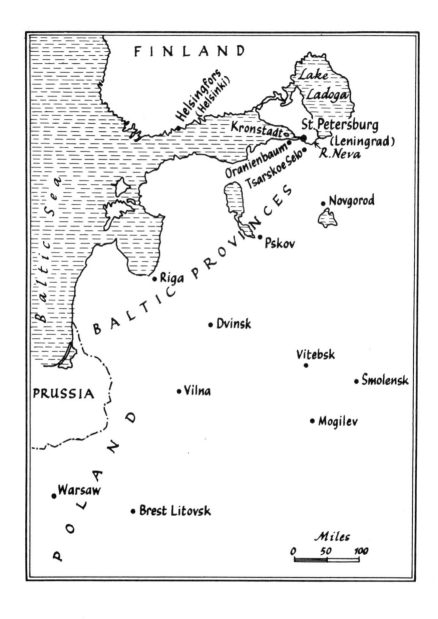

likely to be pushed out again in a few days' time. Moreover, at his headquarters there were French and British officers insisting that Russia must go on with the war.

So he refused to obey the orders from Petrograd. The Bolsheviks then declared that he was dismissed, and sent one of their own men, Krylenko, to replace him.

On November 25th Krylenko with his bodyguard of Red sailors reached Dvinsk on the way to Mogilev. He dismissed the local generals, and gave orders that the Russian soldiers in the front line should fraternize with the Germans in the trenches opposite.

On November 26th the Russians sent a delegation under a white flag across the lines. The delegation reached an agreement with the German Command that armistice negotiations should start the following week at Brest-Litovsk.

Krylenko went on to Mogilev and took over the Supreme Headquarters without any fighting. But the unfortunate Dukhonin was shot in the head and killed by one of Krylenko's sailors.

The talks at Brest-Litovsk began on December 3rd. There were hitches and delays, but by the middle of the month a formal armistice was signed, and German and Russian delegations proceeded to Brest-Litovsk to negotiate a peace treaty.

Russia at this period presents a confused picture. The Bolsheviks were in control of Petrograd and Moscow and of most of central Russia and were extending their power towards the east. But in the south of the country the Don Cossacks had set up an independent anti-Bolshevik government. In the west a similar government for the Ukraine had been set up in Kiev.

Along the northwestern fringe, the Poles, the Finns and the peoples of the Baltic States, who had all been under Russian rule, were now trying to set up independent countries of their own. It almost looked as if the old Russia was about to fall to pieces.

The Western Allies, the French and British in particular, were protesting at the Brest-Litovsk negotiations and threatening and demanding that Russia should continue with the war. But this of course was quite impossible as the rank and file of the Russian Army had no intention of fighting.

The Bolsheviks knew perfectly well that the Russian Army was now of no military value. But they were hoping that their revolution would touch off other revolutions, first of all in Germany and then in Western Europe.

Accordingly the Bolshevik delegation (of which in the later stages Trotsky was the head) made use of the Brest-Litovsk negotiations as an opportunity to call for revolutions throughout the world. They made rousing speeches and issued resounding proclamations. They had printed thousands of revolutionary leaflets to be smuggled across the front and distributed inside Germany.

But this effort produced little result. The Western Allies, of course, were furious at the whole business. The German soldiers at the front and the German workers back inside Germany showed no desire to start a German revolution. And the German military leaders, who after all had won their war against Russia, were determined that the peace treaty should give them the fruits of victory.

The Brest-Litovsk talks dragged on and on. The Germans got tired of Trotsky's propaganda speeches and began to lose patience. On January 18th they presented a stiff set of terms in what almost amounted to an ultimatum. Trotsky went back to Petrograd to consult his colleagues.

There was a good deal of argument among the top Bolsheviks. Lenin, Stalin and one or two others were all for prolonging the talks (in the hope of a German revolution), but in the last resort they were prepared to agree to the German terms, however severe. They believed that to renew the war would be hopeless, and that one result of the inevitable defeat would be the end of the Bolshevik Government.

But other Bolshevik leaders were in favor of a "revolutionary war." They knew the German Army would advance. But they hoped that in the end it would get bogged down in the vast plains of Russia (like Napoleon's army a hundred years before) and that meanwhile the working class all over the world would rise in support of the Russian revolutionaries.

Trotsky took a middle line. His idea was to refuse to accept the German peace terms, but at the same time to make a declaration that the Russian Army would not go on fighting — in other words, neither war nor peace. He believed that this would win the sympathy of all the peoples of the world for the cause of Bolshevik Russia.

In the end Trotsky's proposal was approved by the Bolshevik Central Committee by a majority of nine votes to seven.

On January 30th the negotiations at Brest-Litovsk were resumed. On February 9th the Germans signed an agreement with the new anti-Bolshevik Ukranian Government. On February 10th Trotsky came out with his declaration "Neither Peace nor War."

The Germans for their part announced that this meant that the armistice was at an end and that they would resume their advance on February 18th. There was no real resistance from the Russian Army, and the Germans occupied the important city of Dvinsk without any difficulty.

All that the Bolshevik Government could do was to put out flaming appeals to defend the Revolution and the Russian Fatherland. In the big cities some thousands of workers volunteered for military service. And a number of officers, anti-Bolshevik though they were, offered to come back to serve in defense of their country.

But of course all this was not nearly enough to stop the Germans. On February 19th, at Lenin's insistence, a radio message was passed to Berlin offering to agree to peace terms.

The German answer came back on February 22nd in

Trotsky inspects a formation of Red Army soldiers.

the form of an ultimatum. The Germans canceled the terms they had been prepared to agree to before. The new conditions were more severe: Soviet Russia was to lose all the territories, such as Poland, Finland and the Baltic States, which were inhabited by non-Russians; and the Ukraine was to be an independent state, in which the real power was to be in the hands of the Germans. Berlin insisted that a treaty on these lines must be signed at once.

There was alarm in Petrograd. A decision was taken to transfer the capital to Moscow, where the government would be farther away from the German threat. Secret discussions were held with members of the Allied missions in Soviet Russia to find out what help the Bolsheviks might expect from the West.

There was more bitter argument among the top Bolsheviks. But Lenin all along was very firm that the new German terms must be accepted, and threatened to resign unless they were. This threat was enough to turn the scale, as most of Lenin's colleagues felt that his leadership was quite essential. In the end seven members of the Bolshevik Central Committee voted for acceptance, four voted against and four abstained. On March 3rd the peace treaty was signed at Brest-Litovsk.

After a treaty has been signed it has to be ratified, or confirmed by the supreme authority, in this case the Congress of Soviets. Here there were more stormy scenes. The Left SRs were all bitterly opposed to the terms and they resigned from the government. Several of the leading Bolsheviks continued to oppose the peace. But the treaty was ratified, on March 15th, by a majority vote.

The Treaty of Brest-Litovsk gave the Bolsheviks a much-needed breathing space in which to get a firm grip over the country, or perhaps to start to do so, because this was to be a long and difficult business. After all, the great majority of Russians were non-Bolsheviks, if not actively anti-Bolshevik.

There were quite a number of secret societies which came into being to plot and to plan ways and means of overthrowing the Bolshevik Government. Some were made up of former officers, some of liberals, and some even of Right Wing Socialists.

The Cheka was kept busy ferreting out these secret societies and arresting their members.

Then there were the other Socialist parties, including now the Left SRs, who wanted to denounce the Treaty of Brest-Litovsk and go to war again against the Germans. There were the Right SRs, who wanted the Constituent Assembly brought back.

There were the Mensheviks, who had strongly disapproved of the *coup d'état* of November, and who (like everyone else) were angry at the way the Bolsheviks took all the top jobs and decided how everything was to be done. And there were noisy and active groups of Anarchists who did not want any government at all.

At first the Bolsheviks did not feel it would be safe to declare any of these parties illegal — that was to come later. But they took a number of steps to reduce their influence. Their newspapers were suppressed, meetings broken up, and individual Socialists and Anarchists arrested on various charges. Here again, of course, the Cheka played a very active part.

And then the war and the revolution had left so much in such a muddle that the new Bolshevik Government had a great deal to do before it could start building up a new Socialist Russia. Public services, government offices and banks had to be got going again.

The factories were quite a problem. At the time of the revolution the Bolsheviks, to bring the workers over to their side, had proclaimed the idea of *workers' control* in the factories. The workers had taken this to mean they could do just as they liked, and as a result the factories were producing little or nothing. It proved to be a big task to restore work discipline.

Food was becoming short in the big towns, because the peasants saw no point in bringing in their foodstuff when they could not buy the cloth and salt and matches and other things they wanted. The authorities had to use armed squads to take the foodstuff by force.

It was at this time — in the spring of 1918 — that the Bolsheviks changed the official name of their party to Communists. This caused some confusion among simpleminded people. Peasants, for instance, would say they were for the Bolsheviks who had given them their land, but were against the Communists who were taking away their produce.

CHAPTER VIII

The Civil War

Meanwhile the Civil War had broken out. It was really quite a number of separate wars, some big, some small, that went on in different parts of Russia. But the Civil War as a whole was important, because on it depended whether or not the Bolsheviks would remain in power.

Soviet historians like to make out that the Civil War was fought out by the common people, the peasants and the workers, on the side of the Bolsheviks against the big land-owners and big businessmen. But it was not as simple as that. Many of the common people, including Socialists, were against the Bolsheviks, and a great many, especially the peasants, tried to keep out of the war altogether. Thousands and thousands refused to obey the draft notices, and thousands more deserted from their regiments as soon as they got the chance.

Soviet historians, too, make great play with Allied intervention. But such Allied troops as took part in the fighting were far too few to make any difference to the result. Of course the Western Allies, especially the British and French, would have liked to see the Bolsheviks overthrown. By making a separate peace with the Germans the Bolsheviks had nearly caused the Allies to lose the war. There was the seizure of Allied property in Russia; and the Bolshevik refusal to pay back or even to recognize the huge loans that the Western Powers had made to the Imperial Government. Then there was the horror caused by the methods of the Cheka, and the murder of Nicholas II and his family, of which more later.

But all this did not mean that, after the end of the war with Germany, the Western Powers could have kept on their great armies and launched them against the Bolsheviks in Russia. The whole world was sick of war, and any Western government that proposed to start another one would have been voted out of office.

The first Russians to take up arms against the Bolsheviks were the Cossacks, the descendants of serfs who, hundreds of years before, had run away from the villages and settled in the empty lands along the southern and eastern borders. In the course of time the Imperial Government found it useful to have them there to guard the frontiers against the Turks, and so the Cossacks were confirmed in possession of their good farm lands and given special privileges.

The famous Cossack cavalry regiments became an important part of the Russian Army. In 1917 the Cossacks at the front became war-weary (like the rest of the army) and were quite satisfied when the Bolsheviks made peace and let them go home.

But those Cossacks who had stayed on their farms were afraid the Bolsheviks would take away their privileges, and so they determined to keep the Bolsheviks from taking over the Cossack areas.

They formed an independent government in the Don Province in South Russia; and it was here that three of the most famous of the Czarist generals — Kornilov, Alekseev and Deniken — built up a Volunteer Army. It numbered only three or four thousand men, mostly former officers now serving in the ranks, cadets from the military colleges, and quite a lot of schoolboys. The Volunteer Army was perhaps the crack corps of the forces fighting against the Bolsheviks.

But in this first campaign the Reds (the Bolsheviks and their adherents) were too many for the Whites (or anti-Bolsheviks). The Volunteer Army was driven out of the Don Province into the steppes to the south; and in further fighting General Kornilov was killed. But the Bolsheviks in this part of Russia were still too weak and too divided to keep the area under control, and by June, 1918, the Don had once more an independent anti-Bolshevik Cossack government. By that time civil war had broken out in east Russia and Siberia. Here it all started with the Czechoslovak Legion.

When World War I began Czechoslovakia was part of the Austrian Empire, but the Czechs and Slovaks wanted their independence, and a number of them living in Russia formed a volunteer Legion to fight on the Russian side against the Austrians. During the war many Czechs in the Austrian Army deserted to the Russians or were taken prisoners, and many of these joined up with the Legion.

By the beginning of 1918 the Legion consisted of 40,000 well-equipped men. It was then decided that the whole force should be withdrawn from Russia and brought back to fight by the side of the Allied armies in France. As of course Germany and Austria-Hungary blocked the direct route, it was arranged that they should travel across Russia and Siberia — a train journey of nearly six thousand miles — to Vladivostock on the Pacific, and then by sea — halfway round the world again — to Bordeaux in France. By late May their trains were strung out right across the Urals and Siberia from Penza near the Volga nearly to Vladivostock.

Then there was trouble. Although the Bolshevik Government had agreed, officially, that the Czechoslovaks should leave, they secretly wished them to stay on in Russia and serve the Bolsheviks. Communist agents began to press Czech soldiers to desert the Legion and join the Reds. As the Czechs wanted to get back home, this caused bad feeling.

There was trouble about the handing over of Czech arms to the Bolshevik authorities; there was trouble about the provision of trains and locomotives to take the Legion eastwards. There were various incidents — and mounting suspicion on both sides. The Czechs thought the Bolsheviks were trying to prevent their move. The Reds thought the Czechs were going to turn against them.

In late May the Czech leaders decided that if more difficulties were put in their way they would fight their way to the Pacific by force. And about the same time Trotsky, the Commissar of War, lost patience and issued an order to all the Soviets along the railway line that the Czechs must be disarmed and put into labor battalions.

Then the shooting began. But the Soviets in Siberia were weak, with no good troops and little popular support, and in a few weeks' time and with very little loss the Czechs had overthrown all the Bolshevik authorities all along the line between the Volga and the Pacific. The local anti-Bolsheviks then took over power and set up a number of governments, the most important being a Socialist Revolutionary one at Samara, now Kuibyshev, on the Volga, and another, more conservative, at Omsk in Siberia.

When this happened the Czechs received orders from the Allies in Paris to remain for the time being in Russia. During the summer Allied forces (mostly British) landed in Murmansk and Archangel in the far north. Others (mostly Americans and Japanese) landed in Vladivostock in the Far East. On the Volga the Czechs and the little army hastily got together by the Samara Socialists went over to the offensive and won a number of victories over the untrained and ill-disciplined Red troops. In August they captured Kazan on the Volga with the huge State Gold Reserve that had been sent there for safety. It seemed that Bolshevik power was about to collapse.

Meanwhile the Emperor Nicholas and his family had met with their tragic end.

The Provisional Government, as we have seen, had sent them off to Siberia in August 1917, and lodged them in a country house near Tobolsk. There was a guard, of course, to see that they stayed there, but at first they were kindly treated. One minor trouble was the cold. The autumn nights were chilly and the place was short of fuel. The Emperor spent a lot of time sawing up logs on the grounds. But he enjoyed that sort of work, and in the evenings he would read aloud to his family. On the whole it was the most peaceful and perhaps one of the happiest times of their whole lives.

After the Bolsheviks seized power in November the guards became more severe. In early May the family was moved to what had been the house of a rich merchant in Ekaterinburg (Sverdlovsk), and here they were very much made to feel that they were prisoners in the hands of their enemies. About the time of the Czech revolt in late May, the house was given the sinister name of "The House of Special Purpose."

In early July, Czech and anti-Bolshevik Russian troops were on the move towards Ekaterinburg. The Bolsheviks feared that the Emperor might be rescued and put at the head of an anti-Bolshevik movement. New guards were brought in. A Cheka official was appointed as Commandant.

On the night of July 16th the whole party — the Emperor, the Empress, the four girls, the little invalid prince, their family doctor, and three of their servants — were taken down to the cellar. There they were massacred. The bodies were carried off to a disused iron mine, a few miles out of town; and there stripped, cut to pieces, soaked in acid, burned and thrown down an old mine shaft. But when the anti-Bolshevik armies arrived about a week later the charred remains were enough for them to identify the victims.

The Bolsheviks at first made out that this murder was the work of the local Soviet and the local Cheka; they even for a time maintained it was only the Emperor who had been killed. But later Trotsky revealed that the whole operation had been carried out on the orders of the Bolshevik Government in Moscow.

Meanwhile the Civil War was going on. At first the Bolsheviks did badly. As we have seen, the old army, largely as a result of Bolshevik propaganda, had fallen to pieces: The men had just packed up and gone back to their villages.

So the Bolsheviks had to build up a new army to defend their régime. They had seized power in the name of the workers, and accordingly at first they looked to the workers to volunteer for military service to defend the Revolution. Early in 1918 nearly all the Red forces were groups of volunteers who elected their own officers.

They soon found this did not work. For one thing there

Red guards in civilian clothes stand as sentries to the office used by Lenin and Trotsky about the time of the seizure of the government.

were not nearly enough volunteers. As we have said, most Russians did not want to fight at all. Many of those who did volunteer soon found that they did not like army life and deserted. Those that remained had little discipline. If they did not agree with any order they would not carry it out. If things went wrong they would panic, and things very often did go wrong, because officers and men alike were ill-trained and had none of the technical know-how so essential to a modern fighting force.

It was mainly Trotsky, with the backing of Lenin, who changed all that. Compulsory draft took the place of volunteering. Elections to posts of command and regimental committees were abolished. Strict discipline was introduced. New and strict arrangements were made for supply and transport. To provide the know-how, very large numbers of former Imperial Army officers were brought in to serve in the Red forces.

There were a (very) few officers who were genuine revolutionaries and supported the Bolshevik cause; and rather more who saw the chance of making a career in the Red Army. But most officers were anti-Bolshevik, and a number of Trotsky's colleagues were horrified at the idea of putting these officers into a position where, they thought, they might turn the armed forces against the Bolshevik Government.

This risk was countered by the watchfulness of the military commissars, fanatical Bolsheviks who were attached, with full powers, to all Red Army units. Trotsky ordered that "every officer should have a commissar with a loaded revolver on his right and another on his left." He further arranged that if any officer deserted to the Whites his wife and family should be severely punished for it.

Trotsky first went to the front in August 1918 and set up his headquarters near the west bank of the Volga opposite Kazan, which had just been taken by the Czechs and Samara Russians. Once, a White raiding party came across the river, and might easily have wiped out the whole Red headquarters, Trotsky included. Another time he set out on a night reconnaissance along the Volga in a Red river gunboat; the engines failed and the gunboat drifted into point-blank range of the Czech artillery on the eastern bank. Apparently the Czechs were asleep. Trotsky and his gunboat would have been a very easy target.

The Red troops were still unreliable. One whole regiment panicked, rushed on to a river steamer and told the crew to take them back to Nizhni-Novgorod (now Gorki) two hundred miles to the rear. They were stopped by some Bolsheviks; and the regiment's military commissar, the senior officers and one man in every ten of the rank and file were executed. It was largely by harsh measures such as these that Trotsky managed in a few weeks' time to turn what he called a "flabby mass" into a serious army.

Trotsky spent nearly all the Civil War in his special train — traveling round from front to front. There was a sleeping-car for himself and his staff; a dining-car which served also as office and a conference room; wireless transmitters and receivers; a printing press to print not only orders and communiqués but also a special newspaper for distribution to the troops; and finally two or three freight cars with essential military supplies and comforts for the Red Army — the men were desperately short of such things as cigarettes and matches.

On whatever front or sector there was a crisis, Trotsky, in his special train, would be there to advise, to encourage and to prod; to promote the deserving and to deal out drastic punishments to those who had failed; and to ensure that all — both the military and the civilian Party leaders in the area — put their very last ounce into the struggle.

It would take too long to give a full story of the Civil War. There was fighting in the Ukraine in Western Russia; along the shores of the Baltic; in the far North near the White Sea ports of Murmansk and Archangel; and in Russian Turkestan in Central Asia. But the eastern and southern fronts were the most decisive.

We have seen how Trotsky organized the beginnings of the Red Army on the Volga. At that time the Czechs were getting tired of fighting in the Russian Civil War and had to be withdrawn; and the little army of the Samara Socialists was too small and too exhausted to offer much resistance. In the autumn and winter of 1918-19 the Reds in the East had a series of easy victories. But then they met a more formidable opponent.

Admiral Kolchak had assumed power at Omsk in Siberia

and built up a large army. In the spring he attacked and at one time it looked as if the Red line had been broken. But the Reds rallied and counter-attacked, and it was Kolchak who was beaten. All the summer and autumn his armies were driven back thousands of miles across the Urals and Siberia. His power collapsed; and he himself fell into the hands of the Reds. In February, 1920, he was executed.

In the south General Denikin launched a great offensive with his Volunteer Army and his Cossacks in the spring of 1919. They occupied all the south and much of central Russia, and by October they were only two hundred miles away from Moscow. But here again the Reds successfully counter-attacked. All through the winter and early spring Denikin's defeated armies were in full retreat. In the spring, when he handed over to Baron Wrangel, all that were left of them were boxed up in the Crimean peninsula. It almost seemed that the Civil War was over.

But then the Russo-Polish War broke out. Like the Civil War it was a campaign of spectacular advances and retreats. First the Poles advanced. Then the Red Army attacked and almost reached Warsaw. Then the Poles launched a counter-attack and drove the Red Army right back again.

Meanwhile Wrangel started a new White offensive from the Crimea. In the autumn there was an armistice with Poland, which meant that the whole Red Army could be concentrated against Wrangel. In November the Red Army broke through into the Crimea, and all that was left of the White Army was hurriedly embarked and taken off by sea to Constantinople. The Civil War had finally ended in a decisive victory for the Bolshevik Government.

It had been a grim and nasty war. The country was exhausted and disorganized before it ever began. The fighting armies were frequently short of clothing and shelter and sometimes even of food.

In the ferocious cold of the Russian and Siberian winters many were frozen to death, and casualties from frostbite were often greater than casualties from enemy action. When the typhus came, as it did in turn to every front, the typhus casualties were greater still. There were far too few doctors and far too few hospitals.

It was a cruel war. The fanatics on each side had a frenzied hatred for the other. Each side was guilty of atrocities, and this made the other side eager for a bloody revenge as soon as it found a chance.

In the latter part of the Civil War the two opposing armies had much in common. Most of the rank and file were peasants who had more or less unwillingly obeyed the draft. Most of the officers had served as officers in the old army. Both sides had the same sort of difficulties in organizing their transport and supplies.

Soviet writers maintain that the Reds won the Civil War because the Russian people were behind the Bolsheviks. This is partly, but only partly, true. Most of the Cossacks were for the Whites. On the whole the factory workers were for the Reds, though many of them would have preferred a

Menshevik Government to a Bolshevik one. (It was to the Bolshevik advantage that the Mensheviks and quite a lot of SRs, while they did not like the Bolsheviks, were not prepared to use force to overthrow them.)

The peasants, of course, welcomed the Bolsheviks when they drove out the landlords and distributed the land. But when the Bolsheviks called up the young men to serve in the Red Army, and requisitioned horses and farm produce, the villagers became anti-Bolshevik, and were ready to welcome the advancing Whites.

But the Whites brought back the landlords, and often behaved so badly that the villagers began to feel that even the Bolsheviks were better. There were quite a number of peasants who fought against both the Whites and the Bolsheviks.

An important reason for the Bolshevik victory was that they had a unified command and a central position, whereas their various enemies, scattered round the fringe of Russia, were unable to work to a common plan. The Reds could concentrate against each of them in turn and defeat them one by one.

Again, the Reds had more able leaders. Lenin was a more astute political leader than anyone on the White side, and Trotsky a more forceful and effective organizer.

But perhaps the greatest advantage that the Reds possessed lay in the devotion and discipline of the thousands of Communist Party members. Party members are taught unhesitatingly to obey all orders given them by their leaders.

And they are always ready, willingly and gladly and without any hope of reward, to undertake any task that the Party may require of them — however difficult or dangerous or unpleasant. That, all along, has been the great strength of the Communist Party.

CHAPTER IX

Peasant Revolts and the Kronstadt Rising

By the end of 1920 the Bolsheviks had won the Civil War, but they were faced with many difficulties. Russia was exhausted and bankrupt. The factories could get no raw materials, the railways were disorganized. Food was so short in the big towns that people were on starvation rations. And there was disillusionment as well. People had fought the long hard struggle for the Revolution in order to make a happier Russia, and the state of the country after the Civil War was over made them bitter and disappointed.

A very real problem for the Bolsheviks was that of the peasants. The peasants, of course, had no interest in Marx's or anybody else's political ideas. They wanted their land, and once they had got their land they wanted to be left alone.

One can learn how many of the peasants felt by following the career of Nestor Makhno. Makhno came from a very poor peasant family in a village in the Southern Ukraine. He was an ardent revolutionary and fought against the Czarist police, for which he was imprisoned. After the February Revolution he was released and went back to his village.

Makhno was an Anarchist, of whom there were quite a number in Russia at that time; Anarchists were not only against landlords and factory owners, they were against any form of government. They maintained that no one should have the power to order other people about: There should be no officials and no police. The peasants should look after the land and the workers look after the factories, and if there were any problems the common people should get together and decide what was to be done.

These ideas appealed to the peasants, and Makhno became a popular local leader. At the time of the Kornilov affair he led his peasants into action: The local landlords and factory owners were driven out, and the area became in effect a little Anarchist republic under Makhno. The Provisional Government strongly disapproved but it had no reliable troops or police and so could do nothing about it.

The Bolsheviks when they came into power in Petrograd had far too many urgent problems to bother about Makhno. Then there came the Brest-Litovsk Treaty of March, 1918, which gave the Germans and Austrians the right to occupy the Ukraine. Makhno's peasants, of course, were no match for the German Army, and he was driven right out of the area.

But a few weeks later he came back in disguise and began secretly to organize the villagers. In due course he built up a little army of peasant irregulars or partisans. They started attacking weak and isolated German and Austrian military posts. When the Germans withdrew after the Armistice of November 11th, Makhno re-established his little republic.

From that time until the summer of 1921 he was continuously at war. For one thing he was a convinced revolutionary and always ready to ally himself with the Bolsheviks against the Whites.

But, as an Anarchist, he disapproved of the Bolsheviks because they sought to impose their rule on the villages. He held the peasants should be entirely free to rule themselves. To the Bolsheviks this idea was nonsense; it would, they realized, only lead to the end of Bolshevik power. The Bolsheviks were quite willing to make use of Makhno in times of need against the Whites; but as soon as the Whites were no longer dangerous they tried to suppress him.

So that for nearly three years Makhno was sometimes fighting against the Whites, sometimes against the Bolsheviks and sometimes against both.

The peasants themselves, as far as they had any choice, took the side of Makhno. The Bolsheviks were desperately short of food for the big towns. The factories were working so badly that there were no manufactured goods they could offer the peasants in exchange for their produce. So the Bolsheviks had to take the grain by force.

They sent down armed squads and commissars. They tried to break peasant resistance by setting the poorer ones against the richer ones. But this at first had little effect because all peasants, rich and poor, felt at one against the hated townsmen who had come to take away their grain and their horses. The more vigorous peasants ran away to join Makhno.

Makhno had a genius for irregular or partisan warfare. He would avoid a head-on battle against more numerous or better-armed troops. Instead he would attack from behind or overwhelm an isolated enemy detachment. If one of his bands were surrounded the men would bury their arms and disperse into the villages, only to reassemble again when the enemy had passed on. Because the villagers were for them they could always live off the country. The peasant bush telegraph kept them well informed of enemy movements.

But perhaps the main secret of Makhno's success was speed: His troops were always turning up miles away from where they were expected. In those days of poor roads and no motor transport, speed meant fresh horses, and Makhno's men could always get the villagers to give them fresh horses in exchange for their tired ones.

The ultimate show-down between Makhno and the Bolsheviks came after the final defeat of Wrangel in November. The Makhnovite commanders who had been fighting Wrangel in the Crimea alongside the Reds were summoned to Red headquarters, arrested and shot. Large forces secretly surrounded Makhno's native village, where he was then staying. After days of bitter struggle Makhno fought his way out, and beat off a number of Bolshevik attacks.

But now that the Polish war was over and Wrangel de-

feated, the whole of the Red Army could be turned against
Makhno. And he could no longer count on the same support
from the villagers. His most active supporters had been arrested by the Cheka; and there were no longer fresh horses
for him. They had nearly all been requisitioned, taken over
by the Red Army. After seven months of hard fighting, in
which Makhno was wounded several times, he escaped
across the Roumanian frontier. He died some years later in
Paris.

The Makhnovites were by no means the only peasants to
take up arms against the Bolsheviks. There were innumer-
able smaller bands in the Ukraine (some of which were
merely gangs of thieves). In the Tambov province — between Moscow and the Volga — fighting went on for two
years, and big Red Army formations had to be brought in
to crush the insurgent peasants. In Western Siberia peasant
partisan detachments who had fought for the Reds in the
Civil War turned against them when they felt the harsh
severities of Soviet rule.

But armed revolt was not the only problem for the régime.
Even more important was the sullen refusal of the peasants, all over Russia, to deliver the foodstuff so desperately
needed by the towns. The goods the peasants wanted to buy
were not available, so it was not worth their while to bring
produce to market. When armed squads came out to take
their stocks they tried to hide them. Sometimes they even

burned them. A great many peasants stopped growing any more than was needed to feed themselves and their families.

The new Bolshevik Government also had difficulties with the factory workers. Here again it was the food shortage. A workman's wages were not enough to buy sufficient food for himself and his family: and even supposing his wages were doubled, the food was not there in the shops. For this reason a lot of workmen with relations in the country went back to live in their villages; and between 1917 and 1921 the population of Petrograd dropped by two-thirds.

Even so there was not enough food to go round. The authorities had to start paying the workers in rations instead of money. But the ration, that is, the amount of food a worker got, was not the same for all; some classes of workers got more than others, and these differences led to jealousy and resentment.

Many workers would take days off to go on foraging expeditions into the country. They would buy or obtain by barter anything the peasants had to spare, potatoes, or a sack of grain, or vegetables, and bring it back to their families. But the authorities declared this illegal. They set up road blocks to search anyone coming back from the country; and food found was taken away and the men prosecuted for "speculating."

Another grievance was the Labor Army, which was an idea of Trotsky's. It consisted of detachments of ex-Civil

War soldiers who had not been discharged from the army, but were kept on as a sort of labor reserve to work in whatever factory the authorities might decide. The ordinary workers, with some justification, regarded these people as strike breakers.

Then there was dissatisfaction over the privileged position of the Communist Party. Party members seemed to be taking all the leading jobs. And in all large factories there were squads of armed Communist Party members, under the orders of the local Party bosses, who could be used to enforce the will of these bosses on the other factory workers.

By the end of 1920 there was considerable unrest among workers. This was most marked in Petrograd. In February, 1921, there were strikes and demonstrations at all the big factories. Meetings were held calling for the abolition of road blocks and of the system of different rations for different classes of workers. They also wanted the Labor Army men withdrawn and the Communist factory squads disarmed.

The Bolshevik authorities became alarmed. A curfew was imposed to keep people in at night and street demonstrations were forbidden. Defense committees were set up in the factories, backed by the Party's armed squads. Cadets from the neighboring military colleges were called in to patrol the city.

But there was a good deal of sympathy for the workers even within the Communist Party itself. Many members felt the Party leaders were being too strict and that people should be given more liberty. The danger of a split within the Party was a matter of great concern to Lenin.

Unrest came to a head in the Kronstadt revolt of March, 1921. Kronstadt is a fortress and naval base on an island in the Gulf of Finland, about twenty miles from Petrograd, but only five miles from the nearest point on the mainland, the town of Oranienbaum that lies due south of it. Every year, from December to March, the gulf is icebound, and the way to Kronstadt is over the ice, which is thick enough to bear heavy trucks.

In 1921 the population of Kronstadt was about 50,000. There were a number of sailors, including the crews of two battleships icebound in the harbor, the soldiers who manned the forts, and the dock workers with their wives and families. Kronstadt had a revolutionary tradition, and, as we have seen, Kronstadt sailors had played an important part in helping the Bolsheviks to seize power.

When the strikes and demonstrations broke out in Petrograd in February the Kronstadt sailors sent over delegates to see what was happening. When they came back they reported to a mass meeting on February 28th on board one of the battleships, and the meeting then voted for a long resolution or statement of what they wanted.

This resolution is a remarkable document. It contains all the demands made by the Petrograd workers — the abolition of privileged rations, of road blocks and of armed Communist guards. But it also contains a charter of freedom for all workers, peasants and Left Wing Socialists. It demands freedom of speech and assembly, freedom of workers and peasant unions, freedom of secret elections to Soviets, and freedom for other people as well as Communists to start newspapers and issue propaganda. It also calls for a freely elected conference of all workers, soldiers and sailors of the Petrograd and Kronstadt area, whether Communists or not.

There is nothing counter-revolutionary about this resolution. There was no question of calling for any freedoms for landlords or for the bourgeoisie. It was, in effect, a statement of just what had been in the minds of so many workers and peasants and soldiers when they sided with the Bolsheviks in 1917 and during the Civil War. But the resolution would have meant that the Communists would no longer be the sole rulers of Russia, and as such it could not be accepted by the Bolshevik leadership.

The next day, March 1st, two top Bolsheviks were sent over from Petrograd to bring the men to reason. There were two stormy meetings, and when the second broke up, on March 2nd, with the men still refusing to water down their resolution, it was obvious that a clash was coming.

It is clear that the Kronstadt leaders never imagined they would have to fight against the Soviet Government. Had they done so they would have delayed their move for two or three weeks, till the thaw came. The island of Kronstadt would then have been almost impregnable, and the two battleships (now clamped in the ice and masking each other's fire) could have been brought into action. The Kronstadt leaders were hoping that the common people in other places — workers, soldiers, sailors and peasants — would get together and pass similar resolutions, and that in due course the Soviet leadership would give way and grant what the people were asking for.

However, in an order published on March 2nd, Lenin and Trotsky demanded that Soviet authority be re-established in Kronstadt by every possible means.

Meanwhile, the rank and file of a Naval Air Squadron at Oranienbaum on the mainland declared their support of the Kronstadt resolution; but the other units there remained loyal to the Moscow government. So that when a party from Kronstadt went across the ice to make contact on the night of March 2nd-3rd, they were fired on from the shore and had to return. A few hours later an armored train arrived in Oranienbaum; the Naval Air Squadron was surrounded and forty-four of its men were arrested and shot.

In Kronstadt it was now realized that an armed clash was coming. A defense committee was appointed to take measures to repel the expected attack. But for the next three or four days it was still a war of words. The Kronstadt insurgents bitterly resented the propaganda being put out by Moscow and Petrograd that they were Whites and counter-revolutionaries. They sent over representatives to explain the true position to the workers and soldiers on the mainland; but by now the Cheka was on the watch and most of these representatives were arrested.

On March 5th Trotsky issued an ultimatum. At the same time he ordered the arrest of all the relatives of the Kronstadt men then living in Petrograd, to be held as hostages. Tukhachevsky, the most capable and vigorous of all the Red commanders, was put in charge of the assault force.

The heavy artillery on the mainland started to bombard the island on March 7th, and the attack was launched the next day. But the government troops advancing across the ice were mown down by fire from the Kronstadt forts. Many of the troops had no wish to fight, and a number went over to the defenders. The battle of March 8th was a complete victory for the Kronstadt insurgents.

Tukhachevsky urgently prepared for a second attack in much greater strength. Time was pressing; at any moment now the ice might break up. Everything possible was done to make the troops believe that the Kronstadt insurgents were the enemies of the Revolution. Seasoned troops were brought up from all parts of Russia. There were detachments of Petrograd Party members and of young Communists from Moscow University. There were whole battalions of cadets from the military schools. Three hundred leading Communists came down from Moscow, where the Tenth Party Congress was then in session.

The preliminary bombardment lasted all the afternoon of March 16th. This time there were two attacking forces advancing across the ice, one from the southern shore of the gulf and one from the northern. The advance began in the small hours of the 17th. It was of course still dark, and when morning came a thick fog persisted. A battalion of the northern group blundered onto a minefield: the explosions broke up the ice and all but eighteen men were drowned.

The actual battle began at 5 A.M. on the 17th, and very bloody fighting went on continuously till noon on the 18th, by which time the government forces had occupied most of the town and seized the two battleships. The Kronstadt rising had been brought to an end.

Some of the insurgents escaped across the ice to the north and managed to make their way to Finland. Quite a number were massacred in the last stages of the struggle — some of the attacking units were taking no prisoners. It was later announced that some of those conveyed by the Cheka to prisons on the mainland had been found guilty of mutiny and shot. None were brought to public trial. It was thought that it might be damaging to the Bolshevik cause if they were given a chance to explain their reasons for what they had done.

CHAPTER X

The Consolidation of Power

With the trouble in the villages and the trouble in the factories, with argument and disagreement within the Communist Party, with an armed revolt in Kronstadt and with all the evidence that most Russians were dissatisfied with Communist rule, the leadership of the Communist Party was in a difficult position in the early spring of 1921. The way Lenin dealt with it shows his political genius.

As Lenin saw it, the practical problem was food for the starving towns. Food could only come from the peasant farmers. Force had been tried against the peasants, but these forceful methods had failed to secure enough foodstuffs. Therefore some way must be found to make it worth the peasants' while to grow more food and bring it to the market.

The other problem was political. It was now clear that if absolutely free elections were allowed the Communists would simply be voted out of power. But Lenin had all along been convinced that only if the Communist Party had absolute power could Russia be made to develop into a Communist state on the lines laid down by Marx. Therefore there could be no free elections.

And then the Party must be united and disciplined. If rank-and-file Communists were allowed to disagree with what the leadership told them and to call on others to join them, the result, Lenin felt, would be that the Party would split into a number of quarrelsome groups, and if it did that it could never maintain its absolute power in the country.

In other words Lenin held that Russia must be completely under the Communist Party, and the Communist Party must be completely under the Party leadership (which of course meant Lenin himself).

At the Tenth Party Congress in Moscow (held at the time of the Kronstadt revolt) Lenin successfully brought to heel those in the Party who had been disagreeing with him. He hinted that the way they had behaved had encouraged the counter-revolutionary Kronstadt rebels. This was unfair on Lenin's part, but it made the oppositionists anxious to prove their Party loyalty. So that when an appeal was made for members of the Congress to go and take part in the final attack on Kronstadt the oppositionists at once volunteered.

All this made it possible for Lenin to get the Congress to pass resolutions which forbade the formation of opposition groups within the Party, and allowed the Party to expel members who opposed the leadership.

The other important move by Lenin at the Tenth Congress was the announcement of the New Economic Policy or NEP. This was designed to persuade the peasants to produce more food, and to get the factories working again. It laid down that peasants must hand over part of their crops as tax, but could freely sell the rest for the best price they could get. At the same time people might open shops, and even start running factories.

There were some Communists who did not like NEP. They looked on it as a departure from Socialism and a return to private enterprise and bourgeois ways. Lenin, however, insisted that it was necessary. And at the same time he made it very clear that it did not mean that the Communist Party was giving up any of its power.

The beginning of NEP came at the time of a very serious food crisis. There was drought in some of the more important grain-producing areas, the crops failed, and many thousands of people starved to death.

Appeals were made to workers all over the world to send help to Socialist Russia. Many workers did give up part of their wages to provide supplies. But by far the most substantial amount of aid came in from welfare organizations like the American Relief Administration and the Quakers. Indeed it was only thanks to this help from the "capitalist" West that parts of the country were kept going at all.

The 1923 harvest was a good one, and the crisis receded.

The New Economic Policy soon began to show results.

The peasants found it was worth their while to grow more food and bring it to market. Soon everybody, or nearly everybody, once more had as much as they wanted to eat. More, too, was produced in the factories, though the government-owned heavy industry (iron, coal, steel, heavy machinery, etc.) still lagged behind.

Russia was still miserably poor, but great efforts were made by the Bolsheviks to make the country less backward. Thousands of new schools were opened. They were mostly primitive and uncomfortable: There were as yet no proper buildings, and very few schoolbooks or even blackboards. But the schools began to work; and soon many more Russians than ever before had learned to read and write.

The same effort was made to provide health services. This, of course, took longer, because doctors need years to train. But more and more young people, girls especially, took the courses and qualified as doctors. Literature was encouraged; hundreds of young writers were given the chance to publish their poems and their stories. The theatres were packed. And the young film industry began to produce films that won the admiration of film critics outside Russia.

All this time the Communist Party was making sure that it had the last word in everything in the country. The Party was growing rapidly. In 1918 there had been 115,000 members; in 1920, 430,000; in 1928 over 900,000. When a party grows as quickly as that there is a risk that unsuitable mem-

bers will be enrolled. Some might be lazy, some incompetent, or what was worse some might oppose the Party
leadership or even be disloyal.

And so there were purges, which have so often occurred
in Soviet history. A purge means that the Party leadership
(or a special commission appointed by the leadership) ex-
amines the record of every Party member; and those that
for any reason do not come up to the leadership's require-
ments are expelled.

It was during this period that the *dual* system of Soviet
rule evolved. In most countries today the outward pattern of
government is similar. At the top there is the cabinet; under
the cabinet ministers are the various ministries with their
branches all over the country; and then there are county
councils, borough councils, rural district councils, parish
councils and so on.

In Soviet Russia it is much the same, though they use
different names. But in Russia, at every level, there are
Communists to see that the officials do what the Communist
Party wants. From the ministries at the top to the parish
councils at the bottom, everything is checked and controlled
by the Party.

During the 1920's the non-Bolshevik parties were finally
crushed out of existence. Of course, the Right Wing parties
had disappeared by the end of the Civil War; and to the
Communists it was logical that the other Socialist parties,
the SRs and the Mensheviks, should disappear also.

We have seen that when the Kronstadt rebels called for freedom it was freedom only for workers and peasants, not for landlords or the middle classes. In just the same way those Communists who annoyed Lenin by asking for more freedom only meant more freedom for Communists. Communists hold that the ideas of non-Communists are so certainly wrong that they should not be allowed to be expressed.

For a short time a few SRs and Mensheviks were permitted to serve on local councils. It was felt that this was a proof to the outside world of "democracy" in the Soviet Union. But meetings were packed with Bolshevik supporters who would jeer at the non-Bolsheviks and shout them down. Nothing that they said was ever allowed to be taken seriously.

The end of the Socialist Revolutionaries came at a show trial held in 1922. The leading SRs still in Russia had been arrested, and were faced with a charge (for which some of the evidence was rather dubious) of having tried to murder Lenin. This trial caused great concern to Socialist and Labor leaders in western Europe, who had supported the Bolshevik Revolution but were now disturbed at the way the Bolsheviks were treating the non-Bolshevik Socialists.

At a meeting in Berlin they were assured by the Bolshevik representative that there would be no death sentences. Lenin was angry when he heard of this — he said his representative had no right to give this assurance. But a well-known Belgian lawyer was allowed to come to Moscow for the defense.

This lawyer, himself a leading Socialist, found the trial very unlike any he had taken part in. Mobs were organized in the streets of Moscow to demonstrate against the accused and their lawyers. There were more demonstrations in the court. The accused were not allowed to call witnesses or produce documents.

In the end they were all found guilty and some were sentenced to death. These sentences were, in accordance with the assurance given in Berlin, changed to imprisonment for life. But none of the men were ever heard of afterwards, so they must have died in prison.

The Cheka, of course, played a leading part in the suppression of the non-Bolshevik parties, and when these had been suppressed they turned their attention to all, whether Party members or not, who might be troublesome to the leadership.

The Cheka had Lenin's backing, and worked under his general guidance. But otherwise it was very much a law unto itself. It was quite outside the control of the law courts or of the local Party committees. Some of its members, especially in the early days, were rather dubious characters. Quite a number of Communists were shocked at the brutalities and injustices of Cheka officials and pressed for its powers to be limited and defined.

In early 1922 the name Cheka was done away with, and a new security service, the G.P.U. brought into being. But this was merely the Cheka under a new name, and has remained so under all the later changes of name — O.G.P.U.,

N.K.V.D., M.V.D., K.G.B., and so on. Since Stalin's death the powers and methods of the secret security services have been considerably modified, though they remain an important instrument in the hands of the Soviet leadership.

Nor were its powers made any less. Lenin himself was convinced that the leadership could not carry on without the weapon of terror, and the Cheka or G.P.U. was of course the instrument of terror. Indeed the powers of the security service tended to increase. In the twenties they began to organize their own prison camps in Siberia and the far north, where political prisoners were sent to heavy work on starvation rations and in conditions of slave labor.

In March, 1923, Lenin had a stroke and after that was a very sick man till his death in January the following year.

He had been so undisputedly the leader of the Party and of Revolutionary Russia ever since the October Revolution of 1917 that it was a serious problem to know how to fill the gap caused by his death.

The Russian Communists had always been keen students of the French Revolution, and they knew that when Napoleon came to power that had meant the end of the old revolutionary leadership and of many of the old revolutionary ideas. They were determined that nothing of the sort should happen in Russia.

Some thought, or pretended to think, that Trotsky might try to be a Russian Napoleon. He was the most prominent leader after Lenin. He had achieved great successes in the

Revolution and the Civil War. But he was arrogant and quarrelsome, and unpopular among the other leaders, who combined to keep him out of power. After Lenin's death the top leadership at first consisted of a group of three men — Zinoviev, Kamenev and Stalin.

At that time Stalin was less well known than the others. He was regarded as a hard worker, always willing to take on the essential but rather dreary tasks that did not appeal to his more colorful colleagues.

Now that the Party was growing so large and concerning itself more and more with everything that went on in Russia, Party headquarters appointed committees to make sure that the right Party members were posted to the right jobs, and that they did their work properly. Stalin was the leading member of these committees, and it was some time before people realized that he was using his position to put his own supporters into key posts all over the country.

The next few years were taken up with personal quarrels and bitter disputes over policy.

NEP was working, after a fashion. The peasants were better off than they had been and food was coming into the towns. But the peasants were eating more themselves, and were only delivering what they thought it worth their while to deliver. There were still not enough of the manufactured goods that the peasants wanted to buy. The state-controlled heavy industry, iron, coal and steel, was still in a bad way.

Now heavy industry is important for defense. A modern army needs tanks, artillery and planes. The Bolshevik leaders, surrounded by unfriendly capitalist countries (whom they thought might be preparing to attack), felt urgently in need of modern factories to equip the Red Army. But they had neither the capital nor the skilled labor to get the factories going.

Some Right Wing Bolsheviks like Bukharin and Rykov favored going on with NEP for the time being and building up trade with foreign countries. Left Wing Bolshevik leaders like Trotsky and Zinoviev wanted to abolish NEP and coerce the peasants if need be. In foreign affairs Trotsky wished to press ahead to encourage World Revolution. Stalin developed the doctrine of Socialism in One Country, which meant no foreign adventures till Russia was really strong.

Then there was the quarrel over bureaucracy — Trotsky maintaining that Stalin was building up a huge network of Party officials who were only concerned with their own positions and had no regard for the rest of Russia or for the cause of revolution.

Meanwhile Stalin bided his time and continued to pack his own men into key positions. To start with he allied himself with Zinoviev and Kamenev against Trotsky. Then, in alliance with the Right Wing leaders Bukharin and Rykov, he edged out Zinoviev and Kamenev and scotched an attempt by them to come back into power in alliance with Trotsky. Between 1926 and 1928 all these three were dismissed from the Party and sent into exile.

Stalin, of course, had taken care to remain on good terms

with the army leaders — so as to avoid the risk of a military *coup d'état*. By 1928 he felt strong enough to get rid of Bukharin and Rykov.

Stalin was a vindictive man, and would wait for his chance to take revenge on anyone who opposed him. All his rivals ultimately came to violent ends. Zinoviev and Kamenev were tried and executed in 1936, Bukharin and Rykov in 1938. Trotsky, who went to live in exile in Mexico, was murdered by a Soviet agent in 1940.

Stalin was now strong enough to bring about what has sometimes been called The Revolution from Above. Its aim was to make Russia really Socialist.

Stalin decided to do away with what remained of capitalism — that is to say with those private factories and shops that had been allowed under NEP, and, more important, with those millions of little farms owned by individual peasants.

The peasants were therefore to be forced to give up their individual holdings and to come together in *collective farms* where they would be under the control of managers appointed by the State and Party authorities. Once these collective farms were established it would be easy for the authorities to enforce deliveries of fixed amounts of farm produce.

Along with this collectivization of agriculture there was to be intensive industrialization. This meant new factories, new generating stations, new mines, new railways, to be started up under a series of *Five-Year Plans*, with the aim of making Russia as highly industrialized as the United States, Germany or Great Britain.

The first and foremost task was to build up heavy industry to produce modern weapons for the Red Army and machinery to equip the new factories.

Manpower for the new factories was to come from the villages. The new collective farms — especially if they had tractors and harvesters — would need fewer men to run them than the old individual holdings; so that peasants now out of a job would have to come to the new factories to find work.

Workers in the factories, as also the managers, were to be kept under tight control by the Party, so that the utmost amount of work could be squeezed out of them.

All this, of course, was an enormous task, perhaps the greatest that any government in the world has ever tackled. It was all the more difficult because Russia was so huge and so backward.

It was tackled ruthlessly, with an enormous burst of propaganda and with the employment of strong-arm squads. Party members were sent out to the countryside to force the peasants into collectives. The G.P.U. (the security service) was very busy. The first drive was against the richer peasants or *Kulaks* (some of whom had been employing other peasants to work for them). Five million of these Kulaks were deported to the G.P.U.'s forced labor camps, and a high proportion of them must have died in the grim conditions there.

Collectivization was carried out hurriedly and brutally,

and brought about more misery and loss of life than the two revolutions of 1917 and the Civil War that followed. There was famine in 1933 and many persons starved to death. The desperate peasants slaughtered their livestock (rather than have them taken away from them) and after collectivization there was only half the number of horses, cattle and sheep that there had been before. Conditions of work in the new factories were also very hard.

But Stalin and the younger men (including Khrushchev) whom he had now chosen to help him were not to be put off by the cost in human suffering. The task was accomplished. Within three or four years the peasants had been forced into the collective farms. The first Five-Year Plan for the building-up of industry was in operation. The Communist Party was in complete control of everything that went on in Russia, and the Party itself was coming more and more under the complete control of Stalin.

In the next few years there were to be setbacks and disagreement, and the bloody suppression of those who opposed or were thought likely to oppose Stalin's policies. But Stalin had carried through his Revolution from Above and had laid his foundations for the powerful Socialist Russia of the future.

A Note on Marxism

Marx was a materialist. He did not believe in God or in
a divine spirit. He held that the universe is made up
of things we can touch or see.

He considered that it is the material things that are important for human beings — the food we eat, the clothes we
wear, the houses we live in, the tools we use. And he considered that these are valuable for us only because of the labor
that is put into them. Thus corn has to be sown and har-
vested and ground and made into bread. Ore has to be mined
and smelted and made into sheets and bars.

Therefore it would only be just for everyone to have a
share in the finished goods in proportion to the labor that he
or she has put into it.

But, Marx felt, because people are naturally selfish, if any
group or class comes to own or control the means of production they will want to keep all the finished goods for themselves and leave little or nothing for the others.

Thus in feudal times, when everybody lived off the land, it was the big landowners who had everything they wanted; and they left the farm laborers only enough for them to keep alive and go on working. In feudal times it was the big landowners that formed the feudal class.

But then there came new means of production. There were new inventions and new techniques. Factories were built and machinery installed. And this meant that it was industry rather than the land that became the important means of production. As a result of this Industrial Revolution, as it is called, the factory owners and the bankers who financed them, in other words the capitalists, took the place of the landowners as the ruling class.

Marx held that a ruling class will always rule in its own selfish interests. It will make and enforce the laws. And though it may suit the capitalists to pay good salaries to managers and engineers and lawyers who help to run their concerns, the factory workers (who supply the all-important labor) will only be paid just enough to keep them alive and keep them working.

But, according to Marx, the capitalist age (just like the feudal age) could not last forever. Competition would grow keener. There would be bitter trade wars and slumps and crises. The few remaining rich would get richer and richer; but the poor would get so poor that they would become desperate.

The end would come when the proletariat (i.e. the workers) rose up, drove out the capitalists, and took over all the means of production. (Lenin later suggested this would be a hard struggle, as the capitalists and their middle-class hangers-on would fight ruthlessly to keep their privileges.)

But in the end the workers were bound to be victorious. There would then be no ruling class to oppress or exploit the others. There would, at last, be freedom and justice and equality. All could and would gladly offer their labor for the benefit of society as a whole, and all would receive in return everything required to satisfy their needs.

Marx was quite convinced that all this was bound to happen. He had, he felt, discovered the scientific laws of historical development which made it all inevitable. The question was when it was to happen. But the final and happy state of affairs that was to follow the proletarian revolution was so desirable that it was obviously one's duty to hurry on the revolution by every possible means.

Marx wrote a great deal, not always very clearly, and some of what he wrote seems to be contradicted by what he wrote later. He had no second sight, and time has shown that some of his ideas are wrong: Workers today, for instance, are far better off than they were a hundred years ago, instead of poorer, as Marx thought they would be.

So that there has been a good deal of argument, even among Marxists, as to what the "Marxist line" in any particular circumstances really should be. But all the same Marx's writings have had and still have an enormous influence.

Glossary

Some political expressions are sometimes used by different people to mean different things. This glossary is to explain what they mean in this book.

Abdication: When a King or Emperor resigns from the throne he is said to abdicate. A recent case in England was when Edward VIII (the Duke of Windsor) abdicated in favor of his brother, who became George VI.

Autocrat: Someone who has supreme power and who can give orders to everyone else just as he thinks fit.

Bourgeoisie: Middle class. The Communists use the phrase to cover both the capitalists and also the lawyers, doctors, engineers and others of the professional classes working in a non-Socialist and non-Communist society.

Bureaucrat: An official. The bureaucracy is the whole corps of officials.

Capitalists: These are people who own or control factories,

146

mills, mines and other means of production and employ other people to work in them. A capitalist society is one where industry is run by private enterprise.

Collective Farm: This is the term used when a number of peasants join up, merge their landholdings into one big farm, and farm it as a whole under a manager appointed by the authorities. Most of the produce must be handed over at prices fixed by the State. Any profits are divided up according to the amount of work that each peasant has put in. *Collectivization* is the process of persuading or forcing the peasants to join in.

Communism: The final state of human society which Communists hope will follow on after Socialism. So much food and goods will be produced that there will be ample for everybody. There will be no need for money. Everybody will enjoy working and will be able to work at what he wants to do. All will gladly offer their services to the community as a whole and all will receive in return everything that they need.

Communist Party: The Communist Party of Russia (and the Communist Parties in other countries) works along the lines laid down by Marx and Lenin. The Party aims at destroying capitalism, building up Socialism and going on to Communism. The Party acts in the name of the proletariat (the manual workers), but as the workers are still for the most part too ignorant to understand Marxism, the Communist Party must guide them and prod them into doing what they should. Members of the Communist Party must put the Party above everything else, and must strictly carry out the orders of the leadership of the Party.

Conservative: Conservative should be taken here to mean people who want things to go on just as they have been in the past. (This meaning, of course, does not apply to the British Conservative Party.)

Conspiracy, Conspiratorial: A conspiracy is a plan for action against the government made in secret. See also *Underground.*

Constituent Assembly: A sort of super-parliament. When drastic changes are to be made in the way a country is governed, the whole population elects a Constituent Assembly to decide what the new forms of government are to be.

Constitution: A set of rules laying down how a country is to be governed and who has what powers. The English Queen and the American President have only the powers given to them by their constitutions. When the opposition in Russia in Czarist times was pressing for a constitution what it wanted was a set of rules leaving only limited power to the Czar, with most of the power going to an elected parliament.

Counter-Revolutionary: Someone who fights against the cause of revolution. For a Communist it means anyone who opposes the Communist Party.

Coup d'état: This happens when a government is turned out by force, and a new government is put in its place. Sometimes regular army units are used for this, and sometimes (as when the Bolsheviks seized power) irregular or private armies.

Curfew: This is an order that people must stay in their homes for certain periods, usually during the hours of darkness. The object is to prevent those opposed to the government from getting together and acting.

Democracy: In the West this means a state of affairs where everyone has an equal say in the government. In Communist countries it is maintained that only the Communist Party can speak in the name of the working class (the only class that matters); so that behind the Iron Curtain, "Democracy" means government by the leadership of the Communist Party.

Dictator: A dictator is one who, like an autocrat, can give orders to everyone else. But whereas an autocracy may go on and on, a dictator is usually appointed to deal with some special crisis. Though, of course, when once he is in power it may be difficult to get rid of him.

Duma: The Russian word for the Russian parliaments which sat between 1906 and 1917.

Emigré: Someone who has to leave his country and live abroad because his political views are forbidden by the government in power.

Exploit: To exploit anybody is to get more benefit out of his labor than one is entitled to.

Executive Committee: When there is a large body or council (like the Petrograd Soviet) it would be a waste of time for everybody to take part in every item of business. Besides, most of the members are often away attending to their own affairs. So an Executive Committee is formed to handle day-to-day business, and to act for the whole council when the council is not in session.

Five-Year Plan: An elaborate plan for the development of industry over a five-year period. It lays down what new factories are to be built or enlarged, what new power stations, railways, etc.

Hostage: A hostage is someone held in custody to ensure the good behavior of someone else. When Trotsky arrested the relatives of the Kronstadt sailors his object was to make the sailors fear that their relatives would be shot if they did not submit.

Insurgent: A rebel. Someone who takes part in a rising against the government.

Intellectuals, Intelligentsia: People with a higher education. These terms can be used to cover teachers, university students, journalists, professional men and women who are neither capitalists nor manual workers.

Interrogation: In Russia, when anybody suspected of crime or of working against the government is arrested, he is questioned by the official or police officer in charge of the case. This questioning is called interrogation. The object is to make him confess or implicate other people.

Intervention: Intervention, as the word is used here, means the sending of troops by one country to interfere or take sides in the affairs of another country.

Kulak: A name used for the richer peasants, and especially any that employ other peasants to work for them. Most Kulaks became such because they worked harder and farmed better than the other peasants.

Left Wing, Right Wing: Left Wingers are people who want to move rapidly towards Democracy or Socialism. Right Wingers want to move slowly, or even keep things as they are. In nearly every political party there is a Left Wing that wants to move faster than the Right Wing.

Liberal: Someone who thinks everyone ought to have some say in the government and should be free to plan his own life as long as he respects the rights of other people.

NEP: The New Economic Policy brought in by Lenin in 1921, allowing the peasants to dispose of their produce as they wished and permitting a certain amount of private trade.

Oath of Allegiance: When a new Emperor ascended the throne, people took an oath of allegiance to swear that they would be his loyal and obedient subjects.

Opposition: Those who are against the government in power.

Orthodox: The Orthodox Church is the one to which most Russians belonged, just as most Italians and Spaniards belonged to the Catholic Church. (Orthodox really means "thinking in the right way." An Orthodox Communist is one who thinks as his leaders like him to think.)

Partisans: These are fighters who are not members of a regular army. They get together in bands and get hold of what arms they can. Mostly they hide in forests or in the mountains, waiting for a chance to attack isolated enemy posts or weak detachments, as they are not strong enough or well-armed enough to take on the enemy's main forces. *Irregulars* and *guerillas* mean much the same as partisans.

Progressive: See *Left Wing*.

Proletariat: Manual workers who have no property and earn their living by working for a wage. Proletariat nearly always means the town and factory workers, though peasants with no land of their own who work as farm laborers are sometimes called "the agricultural proletariat."

Propaganda: What is written or said in order to persuade people to agree with the political views of the writer or speaker.

Purge: A purge is a check on the party members by the leadership of a party, when those thought to be disloyal or lazy or otherwise unsuitable are expelled.

Radical: Radicals are like liberals, but in more of a hurry to get the sort of régime they want. They are particularly anxious to get a fair deal for the underprivileged.

Reactionary: An ultra-conservative. It often means much the same as counter-revolutionary.

Régime: A form of government: There can be autocratic régimes, liberal régimes and so on.

Security Service: A police force (or sometimes military intelligence force) employing its own spies and secret agents. Its job is to track down and catch anyone working or plotting against the government. It also has to catch spies sent in by or working for foreign powers.

Slogan: A slogan is a short, catchy rallying cry, or call to action addressed to the broad masses. "All power to the Soviets" was an often-used revolutionary slogan during 1917, and "Death to the counter-revolutionaries" during the Civil War.

Socialism: A state of affairs where all the means of production belong to the whole community. It does not necessarily mean that all wages will be equal: those doing important or highly skilled work will get more than the others. But everybody has (or should have) an equal chance.

Soviet: Soviet in Russian means "council." The Petrograd Soviet was the council made up of deputies elected by the Petrograd factory workers and soldiers. Russia today is officially governed by a whole number of councils from the Supreme Soviet at the top to the little village Soviets at the bottom. That is why the Russian Government is often called the Soviet Government.

Terror, Terrorist: In a political sense terror means drastic action to terrorize one's political enemies. A government uses terror when it arrests and executes those it believes to be opposing it. An opposition uses terror by murdering the leaders and chief officials of the government in power.

Totalitarian: A totalitarian régime goes further than an autocracy: The government not only lays down what everybody should do, but also what they should think, what books they should read, what pictures they should look at.

Ultimatum: This is a demand by one party to a dispute that the other party should submit within a definite time — with a threat of drastic action if it does not.

Underground: Here it means "in secret." Revolutionaries had to work in secret or underground, as the police would arrest them if they knew what they were doing.

Index

155

THE AUTHOR

DAVID FOOTMAN is a fellow of St. Anthony's College, Oxford. A British citizen, Mr. Footman served during World War I in the Royal Berkshire Regiment. His publications include *Half Way East, Pig and Pepper* and *The Primrose Path*. Mr. Footman makes his home in England.